EGYPT

past and present

BARNES & NOBLE BOOKS

NEW YORK

EGYPT

past and present

Texts
Isabella Brega

Editing supervision
Laura Accomazzo

Graphic design
Patrizia Balocco Lovisetti

Graphic layout
Anna Galliani

Translation by
C.T.M., Milan

1 The best known of
Egyptian monuments,
the pyramids - here
we see a detail of
the pyramid of the
pharaoh Khafre -
date from the classical
period and arouse the
curiosity and wonder
of travellers.

2-3 The splendour
and refinement
of the Egyptian
objects found in the
tombs of the
pharaohs, such as
this beaten gold
plate applied to the
wooden chest that
contained the huge
canopies of
Tutankhamun, are
unique in the history
of the ancient
civilisations.

CONTENTS

© 1998 White Star S.r.l.
Via C. Sassone, 22/24
13100 Vercelli, Italy

This edition published by
Barnes & Noble, Inc.,
by arrangement with
White Star S.r.l.,
2004 Barnes & Noble Books

ISBN 0-7607-5984-7
M10987654321

Library of Congress
Cataloging-in-Publication
Data available

Color separations by Fotomec, Turin
Printed in China by Midas

*E*gypt has a long-running history of battles: of the river Nile against the desert, the pyramids against the sand, and of men against oblivion. The eternal struggle between life and death, all and nothing, in a country that has undergone constant change since time immemorial, has been escalated by the seasonal floods of the great river. Steeped in poverty and basking in glory, the country that has vast quantities of both mud and gold, and where life continued into a death with such a rich afterlife, the land of the pharaohs has always been surrounded by an irresistible aura of mystique.

There is nothing more familiar than the pyramids, nothing more enticing yet fleeting than the Sphinx. Built to celebrate the whim of the individual, its fantastic and enigmatic monuments never cease to amaze us. Nothing more than the pyramids symbolizes the unchecked pride, the power-induced delirium of the pharaohs, these children of the gods, who were eventually forced to search immortality underground like rodents when their tombs were plundered by marauders. Sacrilegious hands robbed the royal mummies of their amulets and jewellery, thus desecrating them, in terror that their bodies might disintegrate. Only after they were shifted from tomb to tomb by night with great stealth by a few loyal priests did they finally gain the rest granted to even the lowliest of slaves. Few buildings in the world epitomise so fully the concept of power as the Egyptian ones. Few works of art render the mystery of absolute and eternal beauty like the graceful bust of the incomparably beautiful Nefertiti. Few countries in the world hold such a collection of romantic stories taken from popular legend. Even today's most ingenious advertising guru would be hard-pressed to come up with a campaign that would prove as effective as the timely discovery of the intact tomb of the young pharaoh Tutankhamun, so small in life, so great in death.

Although ancient Egyptians were portrayed in half profile, nowadays it is a culture that reveals many facets of its character, which can be as modern, active and amenable to constant transformation as it is static and conservative. Unlike the world of Greek philosophers or Roman pragmatists, from which it is so distant, ancient Egypt still holds the world in thrall because of the impenetrable mysteriousness that continues to surround its culture, with its striking contrast of light and shade. Blazing gold and enamels, a galaxy of amber, perfume and balm contrast sharply with the sinister darkness of burial chambers that overflow with evidence of former life. Pitiful mummified bodies, black and withered, have been lovingly wrapped in long, white pieces of linen and covered in unguents to preserve them from the harsh passage of time; they dazzle in a glare of jewels.

4-5 Since time immemorial, the history of the Egypt of the pharaohs was punctuated by the life-giving floods of the Nile, the great blue river that periodically deposited its precious lime on the banks, especially before the construction of the High Dam. Since the completion of the Aswan Dam, water is available all the year round, except between the middle of January and the middle of February. This aerial view shows the river at Luxor.

5 top Most of the
Egyptian
archaeological
complexes - here we see
a detail of the great
temple of Luxor,
dedicated to the sun
god - are far from the
towns, in a desert
setting which
enhances their
mystery and
fascination.

6 top left The Nile, with its total length of 6,671 kilometres and a basin of 2,867,000 square metres, is the longest river in the world. Obviously, the Nile has important effects on agriculture, and in the aerial photograph we can see these workers in the fields caught by the first rays of the sun.

6 top right Thanks to the favourable weather conditions, many plants have adapted to the area along the Nile. Among the most common are the Egyptian lotus, the papyrus and the acacia, as well as the water-hyacinth, originally from South America. This has adapted so well to the local conditions that it now blocks up around 80% of the canals.

6-7 The flood deposits periodically left behind over the centuries as the Nile bursts its banks have made the land along the banks fertile over a distance of 20 kilometres, thus making it possible to develop agriculture in the area. Egypt's main agricultural export is cotton, processed during the summer season.

No-one had such a strong awareness of death or a desire for immortality as the Egyptians. Nothing is more fascinating than their firm belief in the afterlife, of which not just the precious ornaments are proof but also the simple garlands of wild flowers, the humblest of the many jewels of the mummies. These offer silent condolence not to the departure from this life of the god, but to the man. These private sentiments, that remain familiar and unchanging to us after thousands of years, bring us closer to a unique and ancient civilization that still reveals a discernible character. Sethos I is not just a name, but a person whose features we can actually observe. It is the personality of the dead men behind the mummies, the fact that they were individuals with their own character that fascinates us. The Egyptians are an industrious people, whose history, swayed by a harsh and inflexible climate, intertwines with that of the Hebrews, the Hittites, the Hyksos and even, according to the most fanciful contemporary archaeologists, with the inhabitants of the fabled island of Atlantis, who were supposed to have built monuments that would have stupefied us not just because of their amazing scale, but also for their technical perfection. That thousands of slaves were sacrificed to fulfil the pharaoh's dream of immortality is an unsatisfactory explanation as to how the blocks weighing two to fifteen tons could have been hoisted in building the great pyramids. Likewise, the ancient water drills do not explain the sublime perfection of the sarcophagus of Khufu.

In our boundless quest to solve mysteries, these still captivate our attention, although we belong to the era of man's landing on the moon, a feat that apparently cannot quench our thirst for knowledge. Proud of our technological achievements, we are unable to accept that such a remote, "primitive" civilization could have known so much, known about astronomy, about magnetic fields, have been able to invent a calendar system, to calculate the surface of a circle or the volume of the pyramid. The ancient Egyptians undoubtedly possessed ingenious inventiveness and scientific knowledge, resulting inevitably in bizarre theories on their origin, that still escapes our attempts at classification. In not having precise explanations, there is a risk of becoming pyramid idiots. According to one such person, the great pyramid could reveal the distance to Timbuktu, the number of lamp-posts in London's Bond Street, the specific weight of mud and the average weight of adult goldfish. Egypt is the country of set imagery and phrases. The Sphinx is always enigmatic, the curse of the pharaohs fatal, the mummies are awe-inspiring and the pyramids mysterious. These are distant images from the time when Egypt became one of the main tourist destinations. Egypt mania is indeed infectious and furthermore it is centuries old. Egypt's seduction of the world dates back to classical times. Herodotus, Strabo, the emperor Hadrian, were just a few of the scholars, kings and travellers who were captivated by the land of the pharaohs.

The pyramids, which were mistaken for huge granaries, were depicted for the first time in 1250 in the mosaics in Saint Mark's Basilica in Venice. Although only merchants, pilgrims, works of art and mummies were to travel through Egypt from the Crusades to the eighteenth century, they continued to cross Europe, arousing interest and curiosity among a small group of enthusiasts and planting the seed from which the prestigious collections at the Louvre, the British Museum and the Egyptian Museum in Turin would grow.

In spite of its tourist appeal, however, the interest in ancient Egypt, as we now know it, began only in the nineteenth century. This was because of Napoleon Bonaparte, who - in 1798 - sought to wrest the country from the Ottomans with a strong force of troops but above all with a retinue of 16 map-makers and 160 artists, geographers, architects and scholars. The studies and inspections of that time resulted in the weighty tomes comprising the *Description de l'Egypte*, a serious publication that fuelled the lively imaginations of contemporaries. As C.W. Ceram wrote in his romanticised story of archaeological research, *Civilization under the Sun*, Bonaparte "won a battle in the shade of the pyramids but the campaign was a failure. It seems paradoxical that the strength of arms has encouraged the start of a new science; but this is how it is. The recently conquered new Egypt was immediately lost, but ancient Egypt

was conquered. The scientists followed the soldiers and brought an unusual booty back to the country: a treasure of new notions".

This is how Egyptology officially started. Boosted in 1822 by the deciphering of hieroglyphics by the Frenchman Champollion, it soon escalated into a fashion and the treasure hunt was on. Whether it was for personal gain, to increase the prestige of their governments, to find the stuff of which dreams are made, or merely out of curiosity, writers, travellers, adventurers and diplomats began raiding tombs and temples. Among these were Drovett, Salt, Anastasi, Belzoni, Rifaud and Rossellini. With battering ram and dynamite, they climbed, collected, excavated, drew, photographed and appropriated bas-reliefs, statues, bronze work, pottery and mummies.

From the mid-eighteenth century, Egyptologist Auguste Mariette was appointed keeper of monuments, to collect and supervise archaeological research, under French direction until 1928. With the collaboration of Gaston Maspero, professor of Egyptology at the Collège de France, research became more systematic and the preservation of the Egyptian archaeological heritage became more accurate. The about-turn came in 1892 when the Egypt Exploration Fund hired Flinders Petrie, the first person to apply a systematic and scientific method to excavation and dating. In the wake of his discoveries scholars from all over the world came and the country became cen-

8-9 The pyramids of the complex of Giza stand out on the desert plane, threatened by the uncontrolled expansion of Cairo. The biggest of the three structures, the pyramid of Khufu, is the only one of the seven wonders of the ancient world still standing, with only the memory of the lighthouse of Alexandria now remaining.

9 top The Sphinx, the most fascinating and enigmatic of the monuments of Ancient Egypt, has always stimulated the curiosity of travellers and tourists. Repeatedly buried under the sand, the great statue sculpted out of a single block of stone is now dangerously threatened by the smog of the nearby capital and the rising of underground waters, which menace its stability and solidity.

10 top and 10-11 The paintings inside the tomb of Pashedu, "Servant in the Place of Truth on the West of Thebes", situated in the Theban necropolis of Deir el-Medina, stand out for the elegance and freshness of their colours. In the valley, which contains tombs mainly from the 19th and 20th dynasties, decorated with religious scenes taken from the Book of the Dead, there is also a village for the workmen employed in the necropolis of the Valley of the Kings and a small Ptolemaic temple.

11 *The tomb of Sennefer, "Mayor of the Southern City", in the Theban necropolis of Sheikh Abd el-Qurna, reserved for high-ranking functionaries of the 18th dynasty, is reached from a 43-step stairway cut into the rock. Consisting of a crypt preceded by an antichamber and followed by a square hall, the tomb is frescoed with scenes of offerings to the dead, scenes of everyday life and, on the ceiling of the antichamber, a vine-covered awning, from which the other name of the tomb, "The Tomb of the Vines", derives.*

trally involved in the frenetic business of classification, excavation and restoration. This culminated in the "discovery of the century" in 1922: the intact tomb of the young Tutankhamun. Since the end of the eighteenth century the emerging movement of Romanticism followed by the orientalist painters had been attracted by the gorgeously picturesque scenes of the east. This contributed to the enigmatic aura of exoticism, of the kind in *A Thousand and One Nights*, that was to enjoy so much influence over respectable nineteenth - century Europe. Yet a dark, sinister shadow was to be cast by what became known as the curse of the pharaohs. Possibly invented by his discoverer, Howard Carter, to ward off thieves and intruders, this story gained credence through a series of deaths throughout the ten years of work spent classifying the tomb of Amenhotep IV's young successor. Even the sinking in 1912 of the greatest ship in the world, the *Titanic*, was attributed by some to the spectral curse. Together with the 2,200 passengers, 40 tons of potatoes, 12,000 bottles of mineral water, 7,000 bags of coffee and the 35,000 eggs on board was indeed the mummy of a priestess of Tell el-Amarna, on the fore bridge in a room beside Captain Smith's cabin.

From the cosmopolitan Alexandria to the minarets of Cairo, from the Suez Canal to the manifest power of the pharaohs along the Nile, from the solitary oases and severe monasteries of the desert up to the Red Sea resorts, Egypt continues to have a unique identity. In spite of the Greek, Roman and Islamic conquests, which for more than a thousand years formed its socio-political backbone, the country of Mubarak, with its umbilical links to the Nile, is still identified in the collective mind's eye with the Sphinx and the pyramids, the magnificent symbols of the pharaohs.

Egypt mania is a virus that periodically explodes into high fever. The initial reaction by the general public to the great archaeological exhibitions and books on the pyramids mysteries, such as biographies of the greatest sovereigns, is always one of great enthusiasm. The splendid pyramids of El Giza have to be defended from the expansion of Cairo, whose sprawling suburbs reach its edges, and the sand continues to erode the temples and secret necropolises of ancient Thebes of the living and the dead. In the meantime, the waters of the Aswan dam no longer threaten the buildings of Philae or Abu Simbel, thanks to man's inventiveness. Yet Egypt still holds the fascination of those first pictures captured in the 36 short films shot in 1897 by one of the Lumière brothers' cameramen. Aided by the opening of the Suez Canal and the railways, these images would attract a bygone world of English ladies and gentlemen to the splendour of magnificent hotels, where they would take tea on the roof terraces. The promo machine was already underway. The transition to "romantic all-inclusive cruises down the Nile" would be brief.

10-11 This view from the air shows the complex of the great temple of Luxor, dedicated to the Theban triad by Amenophis III. This consists of the sun god Amon-Ra, his wife Mut and their son Khonsu. Still uncompleted on the death of the pharaoh, it was later extended by Tutankhamun and, in the 19th dynasty, Ramses II, who added a porticoed courtyard preceded by a monumental façade with six enormous statues.

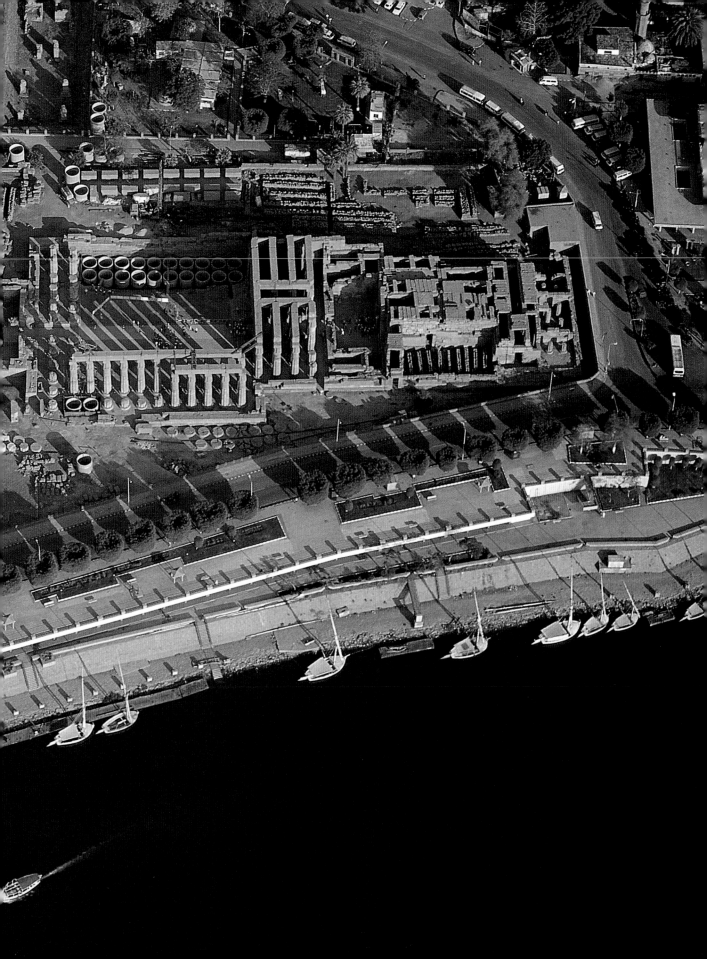

Mediterranean Sea

The Monastery of St. Catherine, Sinai.

Libya

Sudan

Sinai

Red Sea

Alexandria

El Mahalla el Kubra

Port Said

El Mansura

Tanta

Ismailia

Suez Canal

Qattara Depression

Suez

El Giza • Cairo

Helwan

Siwa Oasis

Faiyum

Abu Zenima

Beni Suef

Bahariya Oasis

Nile

Gulf of Suez

St. Catherine

El Minya

Sharm el-Sheikh

Farafra Oasis

Assyut

Nile

Hurghada

Eastern Arabian Desert

Bur Safaga

Western Desert
(Sahara Desert)

Abydos

Dakhla Oasis

Dendera

Quseir

Karnak

Thebes West • Luxor

Kharga Oasis

Esna

Marsa al Alam

Edfu

Kom Ombo

Aswan

Lake Nasser

Hamada

Abu Simbel

The Rhomboid Pyramid at Dashur.

The island of Shadwan, in the Red Sea.

The Nile, near Luxor.

Sea

The Oasis of Ain Uhm Ahkmed.

A view of Lake Nasser, in Nubia.

THOUSANDS OF YEARS
OF GLORIOUS HISTORY

16-17 Thrust forward by the expansion of the desert in the Sahara and the Arabian peninsula, nomadic tribes settled on the banks of the Nile, setting up the first rudimentary forms of agriculture. To the indigenous fauna they added sheep, goats and donkeys, such as these examples reproduced on the palette of the so-called "Libyan Tribute", dating back to 3100-3000 BC.

16 bottom left Found on the Neolithic site of Merimda Beni Salama, in the Delta, this terracotta human head dates from the end of the 5th millennium BC and is considered to be one of the first Egyptian examples of plastic art.

16 bottom right Dating from around 4000 BC, this stone palette showing a stylised cow's head with stars belongs to the pre-dynastic phase, divided into three main periods - Amratian, Guerzean and Recent Pre-dynastic.

*E*ven the name is unknown in its origin. Egypt does in fact come from the Greek *Aegyptos*, and perhaps derives from *Hephaestus* (meaning castle of the Ka of Ptah) one of the nicknames for the city of Memphis, ancient port on the Nile. To the Asiatics it was *Misr*, whilst to the Egyptians it was *Kemi*, Black Land.

With an almost square shape and a total surface area of slightly over 1,001,000 square kilometres, its position in north-east Africa at the crossroads of the Mediterranean, Sahara Desert, Africa and the Levant has had a considerable hand in shaping its historical events. Events there date back to Neolithic times when, forced by the gradual drying up of the Sahara and the Arabic peninsular, groups of

nomadic hunters and shepherds settled on the muddy banks of the Nile, the only ones to ensure a decent supply of water. This marked the start of land reclamation, and accounts for the first rudimentary forms of millet and barley farming, weaving and ceramic-making.

The wildlife, which consisted of hippopotamus, crocodiles, felines and reptiles was added to by sheep, donkeys and goats.

Around 7000 to 5000 BC, the nascent Egyptian civilization, that would evolve from a heterogeneous people of Afro-Nilotic origin with an Afro-Asiatic strain, began to acquire a specific character. During this pre-dynastic phase (from circa 4000 BC) which can be divided into three great periods, Amratian, Guerzean and Recent Predynastic, and on the basis of the evidence of civilization found in the villages of Badari, Merimde and Naqada, political organization gradually focused on small independent states or "nomes". These were principalities of a sort, that around 3500 BC formed the backbone of two kingdoms: Lower and Upper Egypt, which was richer, thanks to the fertile Nile valley, whose seasonal floods then began to be controlled by canals and dams. The main feature of the nomes, or provinces, was an identical centrally governed administrative system, where the first tentative steps in writing were taken. The sovereigns, known as the "servers of Horus", resided in the two capitals of Hieraconpolis and Buto.

17 top In the historic period from the 7th to the 4th millennium, the outlines of the future Egyptian civilisation took shape, the result of a mixed population with an African-Nilotic base and Camitic-Semitic elements. The first tools were replaced with more precious objects, such as this flint knife with golden handle, dating from 3370-3240 BC.

The unification of the two kingdoms is one of the most important aspects of the so-called Archaic Period (3200-2670 BC) and was implemented under the founder of the first dynasty, Narmer, or Menes, as he is more commonly known, around 3150 BC. The first two royal dynasties take their name from the first capital called This or Thinis, and are described as Thinite (2850-2650 BC), the classification of which is the work of the Graeco-Egyptian historian, Manetho, a high priest of the temple of Heliopolis, and author of a *History of Egypt* written in 250 BC under the reign of Ptolemy II. The new sovereigns, who styled their absolute power on the concept of the divine right of kings, as they

18 left and bottom right The Palette of Narmer, dating from around 3000 BC, was found in Hierancopolis. This object sets out the deeds of Narmer, the ruler believed to be responsible for the unification of Upper and Lower Egypt. On one side, the pharaoh massacres an enemy, while the other shows a triumphal procession.

18 top right This lid decorated with two dogs chasing a gazelle dates back to the Archaic Period (3200 - 2670 BC).

were the incarnation of the universal god, Horus, with his hawk symbol, undertook the organization of the bureaucratic and administrative system, and embarked on trading relations with neighbouring countries. Under the Old Kingdom (2700-2200 BC) the first great historical phase of dynastic Egypt began. A major aspect of this was the consolidation of the unified state by a strong centralized monarchy. As of the 3rd Dynasty (2700 BC), Memphis, founded by Menes on the border of Upper and Lower Egypt, became the capital. One of the sovereigns who stands out during this period is Djoser. King Djoser and Imhotep, the architect, scribe and doctor, who was later deified, built the grandiose funerary group of buildings that also comprises the step pyramid of Saqqara. This is based on the mastaba-type tomb found in Memphis, and is thus described after the Arab word for bench.

*19 top right
This statue shows the mythical creator of the burial complex of Djoser in Saqqara, the architect, man of letters and doctor Imhotep, designer of the famous step pyramid, deriving from the mastaba, the typical tomb of Memphis.*

*19 bottom right
This elegant alabaster vase from the excavations of Saqqara shows the refinement achieved by the minor Egyptian arts during the 2nd dynasty (2730 BC).*

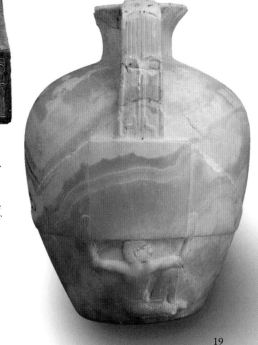

19 left Found at Abydos, the burial stone of Djet, the third ruler of the 1st dynasty, bears his serekh, the graphic element showing the royal palace beneath the falcon Horus, in which the name of the sovereign was inserted. During the reign of Huni, the last king of the 3rd dynasty, the serekh was replaced by the scroll.

*19 centre
Djoser is the best known pharaoh of the 3rd dynasty (2690-2660 BC). He was responsible for the building of the complex of Saqqara, with its distinctive step pyramid.*

20 Khafre, son of the pharaoh Khufu and builder of the second pyramid of Giza, is shown here in this great diorite statue found by the archaeologist Mariette in the valley temple of the pharaoh's burial complex.

21 left 7.5 centimetres high, this statuette kept in the Museum of Cairo is the only known figure of the great Khufu, the 4th dynasty ruler to whom we owe the building of the greatest of the three pyramids of Giza, emblems of the extraordinary level of development achieved in the country at this time.

21 top right During the excavation work of 1908 in the temple of Menkaure, 4th dynasty ruler and responsible for the smallest of the three pyramids of Giza, five groups of statues were found, showing the king between the goddess Hathor and a divinity symbolising a Nomos, a province of ancient Egypt.

21 bottom right Unlike his predecessors, Userkaf, the first king of the 5th dynasty, shown here with the crown of Lower Egypt, decided to build his funeral monument in Saqqara. The statue was found in 1957 during the excavations in the sun temple, built on the orders of the pharaoh at Abu Sir.

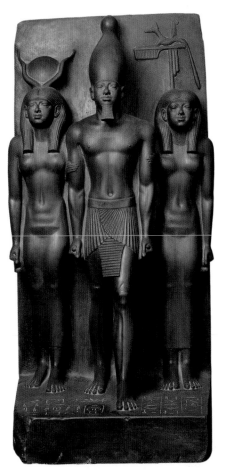

The 4th dynasty reached its zenith under the reigns of Snefru (who was responsible for a series of military campaigns in Nubia, Sinai and Libya), Khufu, Kafre and Menkaure, and is best represented by the three majestic pyramids at Giza. These are considered among the greatest masterpieces of Egyptian art. The 5th dynasty distinguished itself by strengthening the power of the priests and administrators of the nomes, the nomarchs. Under the 6th dynasty the nomarchs took advantage of the loss in prestige of central power due to civil wars caused by the disparate living conditions in the cities and countryside, and claimed an increasing level of autonomy. In spite of the political crisis, however, during the Old Kingdom, Egypt was relatively prosperous. This coincided with the transformation of the pharaohs into children of the sun and the resulting assimilation of the dynastic god Horus to the supreme deity, Aton. At the same time, the first sacred writings appeared, with magical and religious formulae related to the worship of the sun-god, Ra, and Osiris, lord of the dead.

The death of Pepi II, aged 94, marked the end of the Old Kingdom and the start of a long period of decline with strife and domestic weakness, which was known as the First Intermediate Period (2200-2050 BC). Seventy kings in seventy days symbolized the crisis of the 7th dynasty, the first of the three (plus the concurrent 10th and 11th dynasties created in Thebes) to reign during this period of history, which saw the domination of certain Asiatic populations in part of the Nile Delta. The capital moved to Heracleopolis and then to Thebes.

During the Middle Kingdom (2050-1800 BC), with reunification under Mentuhotep II (c. 2050), an 11th dynasty Theban king, and above all with the following dynasty, the country regained stability and power. Under Sesostris III and Amenemhat III, Egypt flourished and enjoyed a period of great splendour.

The nomarchs returned to their status as mere civil servants and the power of the priests was restricted.

At the same time, a period of great colonial expansion took place with development of the Faiyum area, later to become the country's garden, and fortunate military campaigns, that would also lead to the conquest of Nubia, the port of black Africa with its gold mines, precious stones, ivory, ebony and wood.

Obsessed by the marauders who systematically violated the royal tombs, the sovereigns started to dig their own burial sites in the desert.

22 Mentuhotep II, an 11th dynasty king, was the ruler who re-united the country. He was the victim of the independence movements of small feudal kingdoms and heavily penalised by the crisis of the so-called First Intermediate Period. In this way Egypt recovered its power and stability, while Thebes, the city from which the new pharaohs came, began to grow in importance.

22-23 *On this stone slab we can see the pharaoh Amenemhat with Iy. With the rulers of the 12th dynasty, Middle Kingdom Egypt recovered stability and order, while the nomarchs resumed their original role as functionaries and the powers of the priestly classes were redefined.*

23 right *These two grey granite statues show the pharaoh Amenemhat III, ruler of the 12th dynasty, responsible for an extraordinary process of renovation in the country. Egypt embarked on a series of successful military campaigns that led to the subjection of Nubia, with its gold mines, and expansion into Asia.*

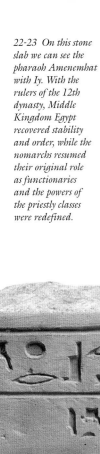

From the Second Intermediate
Period (1750-1550 BC), the crisis
of the 13th and 14th dynasties
(1778-1670 BC) led to the occupation of power between 1730 and
1530 BC by the Hyksos ("Chief of
foreign lands"), a people from the
Asian steppe, who had settled in
the Nile Delta. This civilization was
responsible for having introduced
into Egypt the horse-drawn war
chariot, the olive tree, the vertical
loom and musical instruments such
as the lyre, the lute and the tam-
bourine.

Their sovereigns (15th and 16th
dynasties) subjugated Middle
Egypt and Thebes.

Under the New Kingdom (c.
1550-1076 BC), the country was
won back by Kamose, Prince of
Thebes, and with the end of the
17th dynasty, the Hyksos were
driven out. Under the Theban
sovereigns of the 18th-20th dynasties, who were the first to
be called pharaohs, Egypt enjoyed a new phase of expansion. In particular, under
Ahmosis I, founder of the 18th
dynasty, who was responsible for
ridding Egypt once and for all of
the Hyksos and for reconquering
Nubia and Syria, and under
Tuthmosis I, the country spread
its domains to the Orient, stretch-
ing as far as the Euphrates.

Then followed Queen
Hatshepsut, acclaimed for having
built the mortuary temple of Deir
el-Bahari and for having encouraged trade expeditions to the
heart of Africa. Her successor,
Tuthmosis III, was responsible
for 17 military campaigns that extended the empire's boundaries
to Anatolia. The end of the long
reign of Amenhotep III, who established diplomatic relations
with the Babylonians, the
Assyrians and the Mitanni, and
extended the Luxor temple,
marked a standstill.

24 top and 25 top
A number of
fragments of painted
bas-reliefs from the
southern portico of the
first terrace of
Hatshepsut's funerary
temple in Deir el-
Bahari tell the tale of
a trading expedition to
the land of Punt, the
modern Somalia, in
the 9th year of the
queen's reign. In one of
these, Queen Aty is
depicted with great
realism alongside the
king of Punt, Parakhu.

25 centre This is a
reproduction of a
bas-relief in the
burial temple of
Hatshepsut. A ship is
loading the products
of the land of Punt.

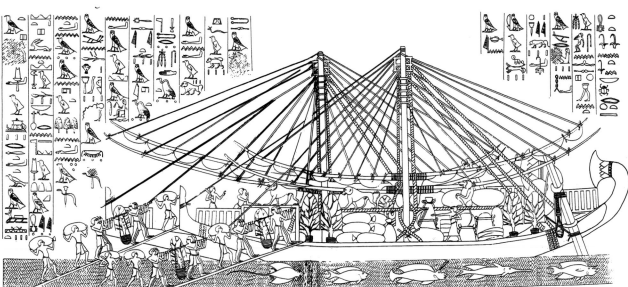

25 bottom left
Thutmosis III, in spite
of the 17 military
campaigns he
conducted during
a 20-year period in
Asia, mainly against
the claims of the
Mitannites, was able
to guarantee a long
period of prosperity
in the country.

25 bottom right
This grey granite
statue shows
Amenophis II.
This ruler, together
with his successor
Thutmosis IV, had the
distinction of keeping
control of the
territories conquered
by his predecessors
Thutmosis I and III.

Amenhotep IV, agent of a dramatic and over-ambitious rift with the Theban clergy, introduced the monotheistic worship of the solar disc, Aton, in opposition to the increasing power of the priests who held sway around the Karnak temple of Amon. In celebration of the sole deity, he changed his name to Akhenaton ("Glory of the Sun"), and founded a new capital at Akhetaton (Amarna). Worship of Amon was outlawed and the clergy's possessions were confiscated.

Increasing Hittite power in the Orient and the signs of Egyptian power weakening in Assyria and Palestine seemed not to have made the least impression on the visionary sovereign, who, in obstinate isolation, withdrew to his new capital with his beautiful wife Nefertiti.

Considered for a long time the first real figure in Egyptian history, Akhenaton, who fuelled the imagination of so many historians and writers, has recently been the subject of some

26 top In this photo we can admire one of the colossal statues of Akhenaton from the immense temple of Aton in Karnak. These statues, with no equals in Egyptian art in terms of the grotesque deformation of the human body, show a man with feminine features, enormous thighs and a prominent belly. These features have led many archaeologists to believe that the sovereign had a faulty pituitary gland.

26 bottom This elegant quartzite head from Memphis probably shows Queen Nefertiti, the wife of Akhenaton, the "heretic" pharaoh. This queen is the subject of some of the most enigmatic portraits found in Egypt.

revision. Although the idealistic monarch played an active role in religious matters, having composed a hymn to Aton that is said to forerun the psalms of David, and to have revived the arts, he was unable to leave a lasting influence on Egyptian culture and society. In his patronage of the arts, he encouraged an artistic realism that betrayed the clumsy, often effeminate, side to his nature. An example of this are the colossi of Karnak.

His twenty-year reign was not enough to change thousands of years of customs. With the death of this idealist, everything returned to how it had been previously. Under pressure by the Theban clergy, who had been restored to power, his successor Tutankhamun, who was his son-in-law but perhaps also his son, made Thebes the capital once again. Amarna was destroyed and the old order reigned triumphant once more.

27 top This relief shows a Hittite warrior. The Amarnian period, gravely threatened by the serious internal crisis that began with the split between Amenophis IV and the powerful Theban clergy, was also marked by the growing power of the Hittites.

27 bottom This Hittite relief focuses on the great military capacities of the reign of Hatti, which began to take on greater political weight around 1370 BC, under the king Suppiluliuma. The Hittite ruler conquered the powerful kingdom of the Mitannites, which became a simple satellite state of the new emerging power.

28 *The golden mask of Tutankhamun is inlaid with vitreous paste and lapis lazuli, and is without doubt the best known of the many finds from Ancient Egypt. Placed directly on the bandages that covered the face of the pharaoh, this, together with the burial treasure of the young ruler, is one of the most precious treasures in the Egyptian Museum of Cairo.*

29 top left This pastoral shaped heka *sceptre and the* nekhakha *whip, symbols of the regal power and authority typical of the god Osiris, belonged to Tutankhamun.*

29 bottom left This fan, found in the tomb of Tutankhamun, contains the name of the pharaoh in the centre. Every Egyptian sovereign had five titles, including the two main ones, the forename and the name.

29 centre This sculpture in the Kunsthistorisches Museum of Vienna shows Horemheb, the last pharaoh of the 18th dynasty, in the company of the falcon god Horus. After ascending to the throne, General Horemheb, who governed during the New Kingdom,

completed the restoration of the ancient balances begun by the young Tutankhamun.

29 right This alabaster statue from the temple of Karnak shows Sethos I, pharaoh of the 19th dynasty and son of Ramses I. He was

responsible for the new and carefully targeted expansion towards Asia. Sethos re-established Egyptian supremacy in Canaan and took possession of the fortress of Qadesh, but he was unable to get the better of his most aggressive enemies, the Hittites.

The 18th dynasty ended under General Horemheb, who came to power through the increasing influence of the army. He was succeeded by the pharaohs from Tanis in the eastern delta, who included Ramses I and Sethos I, who built the Abydos temple and were also of military background. The 19th dynasty sovereigns managed to fend off the burgeoning Hittite power, and after the battle of Qadesh (1274 BC), they reached a mutual alliance treaty with their aggressive Asiatic neighbour.
The 13th century BC was the epic period of Moses, a period almost ignored in contemporary accounts.

Under the long reign of Ramses II one of the highest points of Egypt's glory was completed. The pharaoh, one of the greatest in Egyptian history, completed the reconquest of the land launched by his father, Sethos I, and erected over half the temples that can be visited today, such as the world-famous temple at Abu Simbel. Only with difficulty were his successors able to thwart the designs for expansion of the Assyrians, Libyans and the Sea Peoples. They also had to deal with corruption, economic crisis, as well as the renewed arrogance of the Theban priesthood and an alarming increase in the mercenaries among the ranks of the Egyptian army. At the same time, taking advantage of Egyptian weakness, the Hebrews started to settle in Assyria and Palestine.

30 top This plaque contains the name of Nefertari, the beloved wife of Ramses II.

30 bottom This image on one of the walls of the portico alongside the main portal of the temple of Abu Simbel, copied by Ippolito Rosellini, celebrates the glory of Ramses II, who is shown in the act of sacrificing a number of prisoners he is holding by the hair to the sun god Amon-Ra, who is handing him the khepesc, the Egyptian sword symbolising victory.

30-31 As a reminder of the great battle of Qadesh, in which Ramses II distinguished himself in bravery, the great king is shown in the reliefs of Abu Simbel as he drives a chariot of war, while firing arrows against the Syrian fortress of Orontes.

31 top The epic depiction of the wars fought by Ramses II and illustrated in the haut-reliefs of Abu Simbel shows the pharaoh as he discusses the strategy for the battle of Qadesh with his officers. In the lower part of the relief, among the Egyptian troops, are a number of Sherdens with their typical round shield and horned helmet with disc.
Originally pirates, they were used in the Egyptian regular army, and even made up the pharaoh's personal guard.

31 bottom This relief inside the temple of Abu Simbel was also copied by Ippolito Rosellini. The reliefs belong to the series dedicated to the celebration of the pharaoh's triumph, and show the ruler as he offers a group of Ethiopian and Nubian prisoners to three gods - Amon-Ra, his wife Mut and their son Khonsu are the Theban triad. Between the couple is the deified pharaoh with his head surmounted by the sun and crowned with the emblem of royal power, the uraeus (the sacred asp).

The crisis brewing in the Egyptian realm erupted dramatically during the Third Intermediate Period (1076-712 BC). The high priest of Thebes founded a new dynasty (the 21st) at the same time as a new power established itself at Tanis in the Delta. The unity of the country was torn asunder and the red and white crowns with which the pharaohs styled themselves rulers and which symbolized the union between Upper and Lower Egypt, were divided. Nubia and Palestine regained independence. Several military heads of Libyan origin took advantage of Egyptian weakness and even became pharaohs (22nd dynasty) exercising their power over an increasingly divided country. Under the 23rd dynasty of Libyan origin, a period of confusion started with the contemporary rule of different kings at Tanis, Bubastis, Thebes and in other small states into which the country became fragmented. With the Late Period (712-332 BC) Nubian and Cushitic kings appeared on the scene. They took control of Upper Egypt, founding a dynasty, the 25th, known as the Ethiopian or Sudanese dynasty, which originated in

32 left This solid silver sarcophagus containing the mummy of King Psusennes was found in the royal tomb discovered in Tanis, the ancient capital of the 14th nomos of Lower Egypt on the right bank of a branch of the Nile, between 1939 and 1940. The most important centre in the country under the rulers of the 21st and 23rd dynasties, this corresponds to the Zoan mentioned in the Bible.

Napatan in the fourth cataract of the Nile, and established its capital at Thebes. In spite of the temporary recovery and a renewed phase of cultural and economic development, the country saw the influx of the Assyrians, who in the end seized power and exercised control through a series of vassals. It was one of these, Psammetichus I, a native of the city of Sais in the Delta, who prevailed over all the others. The new pharaoh, who belonged to the 26th dynasty, managed to free the country from the Assyrian yoke and gave birth to what is known as the Saite Renaissance. Under sovereigns such as Neko II, Apries, Amasis and Psammetichus III, all 26th dynasty rulers, works on a canal between the

32 right These gold bracelets from the so-called treasure of Tanis were part of the burial treasure of the pharaoh Psusennes and are now kept in the Egyptian Museum of Cairo. The tomb of the ruler contained four graves that had never been tampered with, belonging to Psusennes, the pharaohs Amenemope and Heka-khepher-re-Sheshonq and General Undebaunded.

32-33 This gold plate etched in the centre with the magic eye of udjat belongs to the tomb of Psusennes. The body of the ruler was inside three coffins - a large container in pink granite, a mummy-shaped coffin in black granite and another in silver - was protected by a golden mask and cover.

Red Sea and the Nile were started and later abandoned. The African continent was circumnavigated for the first time and the use of iron introduced. After an unsuccessful policy of military intervention in Asia, which ended in 605 BC in Egyptian defeat at Carchemish by Nebuchadnezzar, Egypt became a satrapy of the Persian empire.

In 525 BC, Cambyses II routed Psammetichus III's army and the country became a mere province.

Only with the 30th dynasty, of native origin, did an upsurge in national independence take place, especially under the Nectanebos, creators of the splendid Philae and Medinet Habu temples.

32 bottom This black basalt head, kept in the Louvre, portrays the son of Psammetichus II, ruler from the 26th dynasty. Originally from the town of Sais on the Nile Delta, this dynasty from the end of the Late Period, started with Psammetichus I, gave the country, on its knees as a result of internal struggles and invasions, over a century or order and prosperity.

After a brief interval, during which time the Persians regained control of the country for less than ten years, Egypt - like the entire Achaemenid empire - fell into the hands of the Macedonian Alexander the Great, in 332 BC.

With its entrance into the Hellenistic world, the country turned a page in its history. Alexander consulted the oracle of Ammon at Siwa and had himself recognized as Pharaoh, founded Alexandria on the western bank of the Nile and died young.

In the subsequent partition of his empire, Egypt fell in 304 BC to Ptolemy Lagos, who, under the name of Ptolemy I Soter, started the Ptolemaic dynasty, which was to rule the country for almost three centuries.

The Ptolemaic reign, which also ruled over part of Cirenaica, Cyprus, some of the Aegean islands, Palestine and Phoenicia, was distinguished by a period of renewed splendour that also led to the building of the temples of Dendera,

34 top Alexander the Great, the famous Macedonian warrior, conquered Egypt in 332 BC, thus absorbed it into the Greek world.

34 centre
The lighthouse of Alexandria, shown here in an etching from 1700, was considered one of the seven wonders of the world. Built under Ptolemy II, it was 120 metres high.

34 bottom This 1880 etching shows Ptolemy II in the act of founding the Museum of Alexandria (c. 290 BC), an academy frequented by poets, philosophers and the most illustrious figures from the Greek world.

35 top This marble bust is of the emperor Julius Caesar.

Edfu and Kom Ombo. Trade and farming flourished with new life whilst Alexandria became one of the leading centres of Hellenistic culture, hall-marked by a religious and artistic syncretism. Emblematic of this culture were the cults of Serapis and Isis. Yet a new power, Rome, started to loom on the horizon. In 31 BC, with the victory at Actium of Augustus and the suicide of Mark Antony and Cleopatra - the last of the Ptolemies and the undoubted star of Egyptian history to-gether with Akhenaton - Egypt fell under a new master. Relegated to a role of mere province, the country that had been considered the granary of the Roman empire, became the major concern of the emperors; emperors who however respected the culture and civilization of the subjugated country, to the extent that they sought to become the legitimate successors of the ancient pharaohs.

Retaining the right to mint coins and to hold its own judiciary, Alexandria

continued to play a leading role in many fields, whilst worship of the ancient Egyptian gods, for example Isis and Osiris, spread throughout the wealthier Roman classes. Under the emperor Diocletian, the country, considered part of the eastern empire, was divided up into three provinces. The Romans started work on the building of many canals that were to maximize the farming potential of the once fertile Egypt.

*35 centre left
This etching by Veronese shows the death of Antony and Cleopatra.*

35 right The back of this Roman denarus contain the words: "Aegupt Capta".

35 bottom Mark Antony, in love with Cleopatra, moved to Alexandria, where a sad fate awaited him.

With the spread of Christianity, a new chapter opened in the country's history. In 313, Constantine granted freedom of worship to the Christians, who held radically contrasting views as to the Trinity and the nature of Christ. The great Church Council of Nicaea in 325 condemned the Arians as heretics and proclaimed the Son consubstantial to the Father. Fierce dispute and violent skirmishes accompanied the debate over Monophysism and Duophysism, which ended in the triumph of the latter.

In 451, the Council of Chalcedon condemned Monophysism. The decision was opposed by the patriarch Dioscurus, who proclaimed the birth of the national Coptic Church, the native Christian Church of Egypt, which recognized only Christ as having a divine nature. This stance expressed a political rejection of the authorities of the Byzantine Empire to which Egypt had belonged since 395. In 390, the Emperor Theodosius, who had declared Christianity the state religion ten years earlier, ordered that the temples be converted to churches upon pain of their destruction. In 551, Justinian ordered the closure of the last refuge of pagan worshippers, the temple of Philae.

In 619, the Arabs invaded Egypt, and encountered little resistance from the local population, which was hostile to Byzantine rule. In 639, general Amr Ibn Al-As, in charge of an army sent by the caliph Omar, conquered the Fortress of Babylon on the Nile, and thus gained control of the river. Alexandria capitulated in 640 and for a couple of centuries Egypt became an Arab province administered initially by governors appointed by the Umayyad caliphs of Damascus and, from 750 on, by the Abbasids in Baghdad. Arab became the language of the administration, the Copts had to bend to the Muslim faith and the conversion to Islam of government officials was widespread.

Al-Fustat, the seed of present-day Cairo, immediately became an important centre. With the rise to power in 835 of the semi-independent governor, Ahmed ibn Touloun, Egypt enjoyed a revival of fortunes and, in the Islamic context, even surpassed Babylonia in prestige.

But the real economic, cultural and artistic boom occurred with the transfer of power from the Tulounids, who had been defeated in battle with the caliphate of Baghdad, to the Fatimids. One of their major achievements was the founding of the Al-Azhar University in Cairo, which was to become the capital city of the caliphate. Palaces, mosques and bazaars bear witness to flourishing trade, which made Egypt one of the world's most prosperous economies.

Contrasts that arose in the meantime between the Shiite and Sunni Muslims did not fail to reach the land of the pharaohs, which as of the year 1000 adhered en masse to the Sunni branch of Islam. In the meantime, Turks, Berbers and Mongols threatened the Arab world, which had also been undermined by the Crusades. This turmoil was "bequeathed" by the Fatimid to the Ayyubidic caliphate, founded by Salah al-Din, known as Saladin, who was made sultan of Egypt.

36-37 After the Council of Nicaea in 325, which condemned the Aryan heresy and proclaimed that the Son was part of the Father, the Coptic version of Christianity was founded, even though this gained official recognition only in 451, after the Council of Chalcedon, which condemned the notion that Christ was a divine figure only.

37 left Salah al-Din, Saladin I, sultan of Egypt and Sunni Muslim, was the founder of the dynasty of the Aiyubids. This fierce adversary of the Crusaders was responsible for the conquest of Syria, Mesopotamia and southern Arabia, and the reconquest of Jerusalem and Antioch.

37 top right Under the emperor Theodosius I, Egypt with its administrative centre came under the control of the Eastern Roman Empire. In 392, Theodosius ordered the closure of all the pagan temples or their transformation into churches.

37 bottom right This ancient view of Cairo is taken from the Peregrinatio of Bernhard von Breydenbach in 1480. The Egyptian capital underwent significant development first under the rule of the Umayyads and the Abbasids, then, in spite of plague epidemics and popular uprisings, under the Mamelukes.

In the 13th century power passed to the Mamelukes, a Turko-Circassian race, originally slaves whom the Aiyubids had sent to Egypt as their occupying forces.

Excellent warriors, they were the only ones to offer any serious resistance to the expansionistic designs of Genghis Khan and the Mongols, who in 1258 conquered Baghdad. In 1291 they also wrested Acre from the Christians, who were driven out for good. Amid much shedding of blood, the Mamelukes held control of the country for almost three centuries, restoring stability and greatness.

Trade with East and West, and the arts, enjoyed a period of splendour. The sumptuous mosque of sultan Hassan in Cairo is one fine example of this era, which was ended by the Turkish conquest in 1517.

Under its new rulers, Egypt was once again relegated to the status of a province, this time of the Ottoman empire.

The country was now governed by the pashas who still had to reckon with the military might of the Mamelukes, who in the 18th century, were once again sovereigns of an increasingly isolated land.

38 top, centre and top right These etchings show how carefully the weapons of the Mameluke warriors were made. The Mamelukes took power in 1250 and gave the country three centuries of stability and prosperity. Originally servile - they were in fact mercenary Circassian, Turkish, Greek, Albanian or Serbo-Croatian slaves used by the emirs as their personal guards - remained in control of Egypt until 1517.

38 bottom left and bottom right These two etchings, the one to the left in European style, the one to the right Arabic, show armed Mameluke warriors. Even though the Mamelukes were of military origins, and resisted a Mongolian invasion in 1260, they favoured the arts and culture. The first sultan, Baibar, set up a postal service, and the construction of bridges, dams, irrigation channels and aqueducts led to an increase in agricultural production.

39 top The Mameluke domination in Egypt - here we see a warrior on horseback - first with the Turkish dynasty of the Baharites founded by Aibeg, then, from 1382 onwards, with the Circassian Bordijti (from the name of a town in the citadel of Cairo), brought about the construction of splendid palaces and sumptuous mosques.

39 bottom On 22nd January 1517, the Ottoman sultan Selim I heavily defeated the Mameluke sultan Tuman-Bey at Ridaniya in the northern outskirts of Cairo, and became ruler of Egypt. The country, governed by a pasha appointed by Constantinople, became a simple province of the empire.

On 2nd July 1798, intent on cutting off Great Britain's routes to its colonies and at the same time of turning Egypt into a modern state, Napoleon Bonaparte landed there and routed the Ottoman pasha. Thirty-eight months of French occupation was too brief a period to leave any durable trace on Egyptian culture, which was so opposed to France. Battle between the Corsican general's troops and the Ottoman forces backed by the British led to fluctuating results. The victory of the Battle of the Pyramids was followed by the defeat of the French fleet at Aboukir Bay at the hands of Nelson. On 2nd September 1801, France, against which Turkey had declared war, withdrew from Egypt, leaving the country to sort out its destiny between the warring Mamelukes and Ottomans.

The new man on the scene, Mohammed Ali, was a mercenary. An illiterate from Kavala in Albania, he was the forceful leader of the Turkish militia, who succeeded in getting the British to withdraw from Alexandria, which they had occupied since 1807 in retaliation against the new Franco-Turkish alliance. He re-established order, and in return was named khedive of Egypt. After destroying residual Mameluke power by a massacre of almost 500 of their soldiers, he then turned his arm of expansion to Sudan, Syria, Arabia and Yemen, causing an international outburst of protest. Strengthened by British support, Turkey forced Mohammed Ali to capitulate. He was successful in retaining only Sudan, and obtained the hereditary right to rule Egypt.

40 top left On 21st July 1798, beneath the gaze of the Sphinx, the so-called Battle of the Pyramids took place, in which the French defeated the Mamelukes of Murad Bey, who had attempted to stop the invader, thus guaranteeing the entry to Cairo.

40 bottom left and 41 top The British reaction to Napoleon's invasion of Egypt did

not take long in coming. On 1st August 1798, Sir Horatio Nelson (right) of the British Royal Navy almost completely destroyed the fleet of the French general anchored in the bay of Aboukir. As one of the members of the expedition, Dominique Vivant Denon, wrote in his diary, "the eastern army remained imprisoned within its own conquests".

During the battle of Aboukir - to the left is a work by Dominique Vivant Denon, published in his Voyage dans la Basse et la Haute Egypte, *Paris 1802 - the admiral's flagship, the Orient, which contained the treasures of the Knights of St. John, confiscated in Malta by Napoleon to finance his Egyptian campaign, sank with its commander.*

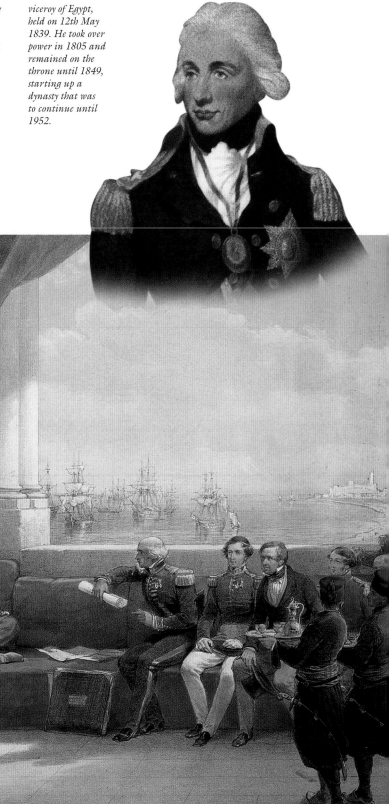

40 right On 2nd July 1798, Napoleon Bonaparte, with the intention of cutting the links between Britain and the Indies, disembarked in Alexandria with 38,000 men. In this lithograph of 1830, we see the capture of Alexandria by the Napoleonic troops.

40-41 This etching by David Roberts (1796-1864), published in Egypt & Nubia (London 1846-49) by D. Roberts & W. Brockedon, shows a discussion with Mohammed Ali, viceroy of Egypt, held on 12th May 1839. He took over power in 1805 and remained on the throne until 1849, starting up a dynasty that was to continue until 1952.

*42 top left Ismail
Pasha Ayyub was the
corrupt governor of
Egypt who was
replaced by Colonel
Charles George
Gordon. When Ismail
was deposed in June
1879, Gordon wrote,
"Don't cry over
Ismail Pasha, he's a
philosopher and he has
lots of money. He set
himself important
aims and he's failed...
I'm one of those he
deceived, but I bear
him no grudge. It's a
blessing for Egypt that
he's gone".*

*42 bottom left
The Frenchman
Ferdinand de Lesseps
designed the Suez
Canal and founded
the Universal Canal
Company.*

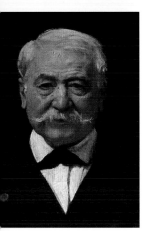

*42-43 top Work on
the Suez Canal
started in 1859 and
took a decade to
complete. The
construction of the
canal, which led to
such enormous debts
that the European
powers used this as an
excuse to place the
Egyptian government
under control, was
opposed by the British,
who feared the possible
damage that its
completion might
cause to the monopoly
they held in sea traffic
with the Indies.*

Until his death in 1849, Mohammed Ali strove to bring Egypt into line with the times. He was responsible for reorganizing the police force and the civil service, developing agriculture, introducing cotton (which between 1862 and 1865 underwent a real boom) and encouraging intensive production.

With the aid of European staff, arms factories and spinning-mills were also opened, and an important civil infrastructure was built.

This was accompanied by quantum leaps in the fields of health and education, all of which launched Egypt on the road to modernisation.

A BIRDS EYE VIEW
OF
THE SUEZ CANAL.

These objectives were also pursued by his successors, especially Ismail Pasha (1836-1879). In spite of the expansion of cotton and sugar production, Egyptian finances, which were placed under considerable strain by a treaty of free trade that eliminated economic protection, became steeped in debt.

The building of the Suez Canal, which ended in 1869, accelerated the country's inevitable economic dependence on European powers. Whilst the achievement on the one hand marked the return of Egypt as a monumental port commanding entrance to the East Indies, the massive debts contracted to support its building placed Egyptian finances under Anglo-French protec-

tion. Because of the national deficit, Great Britain managed to purchase 176,000 shares in the Canal Company, and together France and Britain even managed to have their fellow countrymen appointed ministers for finance and public works. At the national protest to this situation, British troops occupied Cairo, and in 1882 established their supremacy on the Nile valley.

42-43 bottom This map showing Egypt crossed by the Suez Canal was a supplement to The Graphic of 2nd September 1882. The construction of the canal restored to Egypt its role as a major stopping-place on the route to the Indies and increased the country's international prestige.

43 This period print shows the battle of Tell el Kebir, which took place on 13th September 1882. On this occasion, the British troops needed only a couple of hours to overcome the Egyptian army led by Colonel Ahmed Orabi, who had started up a nationalist revolt in Alexandria in 1881.

In 1902 the first Aswan Dam was opened. This was designed to contain the course of the Nile, and was built of local granite.

It was 41.5 metres high, 27 wide and 1,962 metres long. It was extended twice, then replaced in 1971 by the High Dam, built by joint Soviet and Egyptian engineers and funded by the USSR.

It was also at this time that the undisputed star of Egyptian archaeology took the stage, with the discovery of the tomb of Tutankhamun.

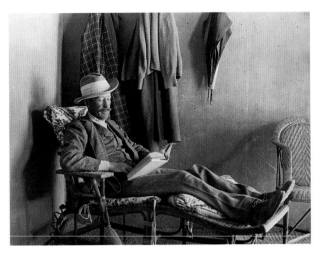

45 left Lord
Carnarvon was
involved in the
discovery of the tomb
of Tutankhamun in
1922. The costly
excavation work in
the Valley of the
Kings (in the
photograph below),
financed by the
British lord, had
begun seven years
earlier, without
producing
outstanding results.
Carnarvon was on
the point of giving up
when the steps leading
to the tomb of the
young pharaoh were
found while exploring
the houses of the
workers employed on
the construction of the
tomb of Ramses IV.

45 top right
Carter and one of his
assistants, Callender,
open the four gilded
wooden chests which
contained the
quartzite tomb and
the three coffins that
contained the
mummy of
Tutankhamun.

45 bottom right
The objects contained
in Tutankhamun's
tomb were stowed
away and piled up in
a rather disorderly
manner in relatively
confined spaces.
The antichamber
alone, here
photographed at the
moment of its
discovery, contained
four dismantled
carriages and two
gold-plated ritual
beds, and it took
nearly two months to
empty it completely.

By sheer good fortune, this had
eluded grave robbers in ancient times
- if only partially - as well as the systematic researches of the archaeologists. It was unearthed in 1922 in the
Valley of the Kings by Howard
Carter, financed by Lord Carnarvon.
It took no less than ten years of work
to completely free the last resting
place of this obscure successor to the
great Amenophis IV.

44 bottom
Insufficient to deal
with the downstream
irrigation, the so-
called Old Dam was
raised between 1908
and 1912, and again
between 1929 and
1934, then replaced
with the High Dam
(es-Sadd el-Aali) in
1971.

Until 1914, the country continued to be an Ottoman province in name governed by viceroys, albeit under European protection.

In that year, however, Egypt freed itself of Turkish rule, and was declared a British protectorate.

This continued until 1922 when, also as a result of pressure by the Wafd nationalist movement led by Saad Zaghul, independence was declared, although British forces were to occupy and run the country until

46 top left Saad Zaghul, a pro-British functionary, became leader of the nationalist movement (Wafd) in 1919 and worked for Egyptian independence.

46 top right The extremely wealthy King Fuad owned a seventh of all the arable land in the country.

46 centre When Fuad's son Farouk ascended to the throne at 16 years of age, he had never seen Luxor or visited the pyramids. He grew up in a kind of isolation for reasons of security, and was known for his passion for women, gambling, fast cars and food. Deposed in the coup d'état of 1952, he died in Italy in 1965.

46 bottom In this meeting of the Arab League, discussion took place on the Palestinian question. As a member of the League, and on the occasion of the vote on the United Nations resolution for the division of Palestine, Egypt, which had only recently become a member of the UN, voted against.

47 top This photo taken on 12th September 1952 shows the first sitting of the government born from the coup organised by the Free Officers on the night of 22nd and 23rd July 1952. The chairman of the meeting was Muhammad Neguib (1901-1984), who was replaced by Colonel Nasser in 1954.

1956, and a constitutional monarch was established.

In 1922 King Fuad I, (1922-1936), son of Khedive Ismail, was enthroned. He was succeeded by Farouk, (1936-1952), between the two world wars.

At the end of the Second World War, set on staking out a role for itself in the international arena, Egypt supported and chaired the creation of the Arab League in 1945.

It was also one of the founders of

the United Nations.

The humiliating defeat in the war declared by the Arab states in 1948 against the newly created state of Israel, further to the UN's partition of Palestine into two areas, led to a military coup. On 23rd July 1952, with no loss of lives, the militia took power and forced the floundering Farouk into exile.

47 centre In this photo, Sadat signs the proclamation of the republic created on 19th June 1953, watched by Neguib, who was to become the first president, and the members of the Revolutionary Command Council.

47 bottom Generals Neguib and Nasser parade in the streets of Cairo in February 1954.

Once the constitution had been proclaimed and the political parties dissolved, the birth of the Republic was announced in 1953 under general Mohammed Neguib. Strong opposition by the integralist "Muslim Brothers" formed in 1928 led to his fall and to his replacement in power in 1954 with the Prime Minister Colonel Gamal Abdal Nasser (1918-1970) who, two years later, also became president.

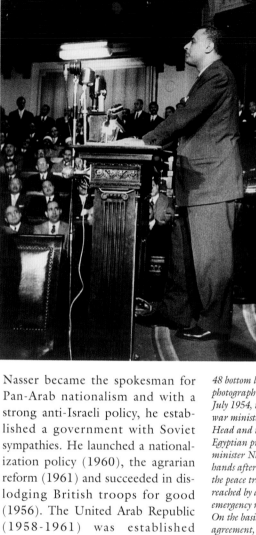

Nasser became the spokesman for Pan-Arab nationalism and with a strong anti-Israeli policy, he established a government with Soviet sympathies. He launched a nationalization policy (1960), the agrarian reform (1961) and succeeded in dislodging British troops for good (1956). The United Arab Republic (1958-1961) was established through the union of Egypt and Syria. The crisis over the Suez Canal (1956), which was nationalized to finance the building of the Aswan Dam (officially opened in 1971), for which the International Bank for Development funds had been blocked by the USA and Great Britain, led Nasser to seek increasing support from the USSR. The dictator's prestige suffered a severe blow as a result of the Six-Day War with Israel in June 1967, which led to the loss of the Sinai. Nasser died in 1970 and the burden of his heritage fell to Anwar Sadat.

49 left These two photographs show the monumental work on the construction of the Great Dam of Aswan. Above we see a stage in the shifting of the temples of Abu Simbel, which would otherwise have been hopelessly immersed in the waters of the Nile. Below, an aerial view of the dam building site.

49 top right On 18th January 1963, President Nasser accompanied by Russian experts officially opens the building work on the Aswan Dam, completed with a contribution of capital from the Soviet Union.

49 centre right Some Egyptian soldiers, captured by the Israelis, are taken to a prison camp.
One of the low points in the Nasser regime was the disastrous Six-Day War against Israel in 1967 when he was supported by Syria and Jordan. The losses suffered during the conflict over the thorny "Palestinian question" were compensated sic years later by military gains made by Egypt in the Yom Kippur War that laid down the basis for the peace negotiations that followed.

49 bottom right Nasser died in September 1970, aged only 52, leaving his successor and ex-comrade in arms Sadat with a burdensome heritage. The funeral became a great popular homage to the memory of the general.

The new president accepted American offers of mediation and with the Camp David agreement of 1978 and the Washington peace treaty a year later he signalled the end of hostilities with Israel, obtaining the return of the Sinai. This event was seen as betrayal by the Arab world and led to Egypt's isolation and to an escalation of domestic opposition. Further to the creation of a free market economy and the opening of the country to western investors, the President was assassinated by Muslim

extremists in 1981. Although Sadat's successor, Hosni Mubarak, continued Sadat's policy towards America, he worked to restore relations with the Arab countries, and instigated dialogue with the opposition. The Palestinian problem, the Lebanese conflict, the Iran-Iraq War and the Gulf War, which occurred at the same time as the disintegration of the Soviet block, enabled Egypt to continue being a part of the Islamic world, but independently. The rest is yet to come.

50 centre right and bottom With the treaty of Camp David, signed in the White House in September 1978 by Sadat and the Israeli president Begin in the presence of the American President Carter - a treaty for which the American envoy Henry Kissinger had worked as intermediary - the conflict with Israel was concluded and Egypt recovered the Sinai peninsula.

51 left Disapproved of by the Arab world, Sadat fell victim to an assassination attempt organised by a command of rebel soldiers associated with the integralist sect of the Muslim Brotherhood during a military parade on 6th October 1981 to celebrate the 8th anniversary of the Yom Kippur War. The photograph shows a scene from the funeral, which took place on 10th October 1981.

51 top right President Mubarak, Prime Minister and successor to Sadat, was elected in October 1981 and re-elected in 1987. In 1990 the assassination of the president of the Egyptian parliament marked the return of the Islamic fundamentalists, a crucial problem in this country torn by corruption and threatened by chaotic, uncontrolled development.

51 bottom right After the withdrawal of the Israeli troops, a group of Egyptian officers raise the national flag over Taba, returned to the country in 1989 as a result of international arbitration. Behind them is the luxurious Hotel Sonesta, currently 100 metres from the border between Egypt and Israel.

JOURNEY IN THE NILE VALLEY

Before Egypt was the River Nile. The history of this nation is written in the blue ink of the great river that has flowed during all its great events. The 6,671 kilometres of the Nile make it the longest river in the world; it cuts through the country, forming a constant, irreplaceable feature on the landscape.

Egypt's unforgettable grey and heliotrope sunsets and sweet, acacia-scented breezes contrast with the silken, shifting dunes. They also attenuate the heat of chaotic cities, colour the small muddy villages and give depth and profile to temples that appear as a mirage in the dust.

The gentle flight of the ibis creates harmony between past and present, whilst the limpid gold of the crocodiles' eyes shines in Lake Nasser.

Along the banks of the Nile, day after day, year after year, the elegant feluccas unfurl their white sails, and old bare-breasted fishermen abandon the ropes that have hardened their hands.

Women past the bloom of youth scrutinize the end of long hours of solitude. Washerwomen bent by hard work, and the children who as yet know nothing of life, paddle in the same water that accompanied the dreams of the great kings and their voyage through time.

The Nile is life, the Nile is all. Twisting and winding its way through the landscape, it has reigned supreme in a desert land,

making it fertile with its summer floods and leaving on its banks, not only its silt, but a past rich in history – a history that could easily be reconstructed by sailing up the river of a country so closely associated with oases and the crossroads of continents. From the cataract of Aswan, which marks the beginning of the Egyptian oasis, the one-hundred-and-sixty-kilometre long Delta bordered by marshy lakes, dams, locks and cultivated land, flows into a myriad of rivulets and canals.

This is the current that springs from below the Equator from internal lakes.

Together with water hyacinths and sycamores, it reflects the most attractive and impressive monuments of antiquity.

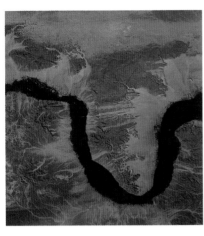

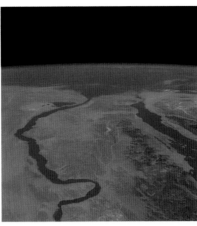

53 top These satellite photographs show the course of the great river, including the Nile at Luxor (left) and the Delta (right), produced by the meeting of the White Nile, with its source in the Ruwenzori massif, and the Blue Nile, which springs from the high plains of Ethiopia. The population is generally concentrated in the cultivated areas of the Nile Valley, the Delta, the oases, along some coastal stretches and in the big cities such as Alexandria or, above all, Cairo, the capital afflicted by smog, chaos and overcrowding.

54 top left Capital of the Hellenic world and second city of the Roman empire, Alexandria boasts many signs of its illustrious past, such as the column of Pompey.

54 bottom left Alexandria has always been a meeting point of cultures, each welcomed to give birth to something unique. The picture shows a sphinx guarding the city.

54 right The Graeco-Roman Museum of Alexandria contains some important examples of Alexandrian art, such as this black stone head.

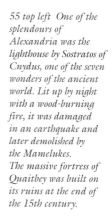

55 top left One of the splendours of Alexandria was the lighthouse by Sostratos of Cnydus, one of the seven wonders of the ancient world. Lit up by night with a wood-burning fire, it was damaged in an earthquake and later demolished by the Mamelukes. The massive fortress of Quaitbey was built on its ruins at the end of the 15th century.

55 top right The catacombs of Kom esh-Shuqafa, in the southern part of Alexandria, consist of a vast underground structure over three levels, from the 1st-2nd centuries. The decoration is particularly interesting, an extraordinary fusion of Egyptian, Hellenic and Roman cultures.

54-55 The port complex of Alexandria, though no longer as important as it was in the 18th and 19th centuries when its 2,000 ships per year made it the fourth busiest in terms of traffic, after Istanbul, Marseilles and Genoa, continues to play a key role in the Egyptian economy.

Arrival by sea at the first port of destination in Egypt offers the traveller, with his expectations of ancient grandeur, a relaxing Mediterranean and cosmopolitan view. Little of present-day Alexandria founded in 331 by Alexander the Great, who is also buried there, completely satisfies the tourist's eagerness to come face to face with past splendour. The legendary capital of the Hellenistic world and second city of the Roman empire defies precise attempts at classification. It has always been a melting pot of different cultures with a European heart, but it has not lost its soul or its sense of history. In the shadow of the famous library and museum and the prestigious cultural institutes, one can imagine the historic events that saw the birth of geometry, the translation of the Old Testament, medical progress, Euclid, the painter Apelle and the physicist Erasistratus. This is how the beacon of Alexandrian culture illuminated the entire Mediterranean. The splendour of the Ptolemies was followed by long centuries of torpor. After the upheaval created by Mohammed Ali, and with the birth of the cotton trade in the nineteenth century came French, British, Greek, Hebrews, Levantines and Italians. This has given the city that Mediterranean flavour that justifies the nickname, Bride of the Sea, given to it by the Egyptians. Its palm-lined boulevards, buildings with wrought iron balconies and Italianate decorations, its elegant promenade, the Corniches, its yacht club, casino, night life and beaches such as Montaza and Maamoura, certainly bring it closer to a Mediterranean way of life. Its beaches were once teeming with cabins and bathers, many of whom have gone to the nearby Agami, the country's Saint Tropez, with its astronomically priced villas. The bathing tradition of Egypt's second city is also old. Although its two ports no longer have the same importance as that reached between the nineteenth and twentieth centuries, its heavy industries still give it significant status in the country's economy. What was considered one of the Seven Wonders of the World, the Pharos of Alexandria, was destroyed. On its ruins at the end of the fifteenth century was built the massive Quaitbey fort, now a naval museum. The huge library of Ptolemy I Soter is now reduced to ashes, and the famous Serapeum conserves only the pink granite Pompey. Yet the city can still reveal the remains of all its former splendour to visitors. The 2nd century horse-shaped Roman theatre in white and grey marble at Kom ed-Dik, the ruins of Caesareum, the temple built by Cleopatra to honour Mark Antony, the Anfushi Tombs and the catacombs of Kom esh-Shuqafa are all examples of the combination of Egyptian and Graeco-Roman style. Much of ancient Alexandria lies buried like its many mosques, such as the one at Abu al-Abba al-Mursi. One of the city's gems is its archaeological museum with its Graeco-Roman exhibits revealing much of the Alexandrian culture, the syncretic result of Egyptian, Hellenistic and Roman civilization.

Aboukir on Alexandria's eastern coast preserves little trace of the ancient Canopus, which developed around the tomb of Canobus, the mythical driver of Menelaus, whereas Tanta, the largest city of the Delta, midway between Alexandria and Cairo, houses the mausoleum of the country's greatest Muslim saint, Sayyed Ahmed al-Badawi, who died in 1276. However, one needs to go to Rosetta to find a place that can live up to a visitor's expectations of a trip to Egypt. It is full of examples of Ottoman architecture, above all the ancient two or three-storey houses in bricks jutting out on to the streets like those in nearby Damietta on the other branch of the Nile. This centre on the eastern mouath of the river is famous for its textile industry and has carved out a place of its own in the country's history. The key that enabled Champollion to shed light on ancient Egyptian civi-

lization was discovered here in 1799. The famous Rosetta stone, now in the British Museum, inscribed with a bilingual decree by Ptolemy V in hieroglyphic and demotic Egyptian and Greek led scholars to conclude that the script of ancient Egypt was composed of phonetic symbols and ideograms.

Once past Tanis, the ancient capital of the 21st and 22nd dynasties, with its royal necropolis, remaining citadel walls and temples, and having left behind the Canal with its lively cities of Suez, Ismailia and Port Said, the Nile leads into the very heart of Egyptian civilization.

*56 top left
Corresponding to the biblical town of Zoan, Tanis was built on the right bank of a branch of the Nile. Among its main monuments were the great temple, facing from east to west, of which a great many fragments of obelisks remain, columns in the form of palm trees, sandstone statues and huge blocks of stone.*

56 bottom left Among the fragments occupying the area where once there stood the great temple of Tanis, dedicated to Amon and discovered by Mariette between 1859 and 1864, are three colossal statues of Ramses II.

*56 top right
Tanis, which stands isolated in the centre of a vast plain, underwent major development under Psusenne I, who transformed it into a copy of Karnak.*

*56 bottom right
The golden collar with royal scrolls and 14 chains, weighing a total of 6 kilos, belongs to the treasure of Psusenne I, and bears witness to the richness achieved by the town of Tanis.*

57 The golden mask that covered the mummy of Psusennes, found in the royal cemetery discovered between 1939 and 1940 near the ruins of the ancient city of Tanis, in the Delta. The crypt, without the external structure that contained the royal remains, threatened by dampness, isn't always visible.

58 top left Smog veils the skyscrapers of Cairo, the biggest city in Africa.

58 bottom left The Khan el-Khalili, (the photograph shows one of its water-sellers), is one of the favourite bazaars with tourists, and takes its name from the remains of a khan (warehouse) built in 1292 by the sultan El-Ashraf Khalil.

58-59 The city of Cairo, meeting point of the Arabic and European worlds, has 15 million inhabitants.

59 top left Built between 1824 and 1848 as an imitation of the mosques of Istanbul, the mosque of Mohammed Ali was completed in 1857 by his son Said Pasha.

59 top right The traffic on the modern Kasr El-Nile Bridge is always chaotic. The city, under the assault of an incredible growth in building work, suffers from the problems typical of all the great metropoli of the world.

58 right Next to one another at the foot of the Citadel of Cairo are the austere mosque of Sultan Hassan - considered a masterpiece of Arabic art - and the modern mosque of Al-Rifai.

Unlike Alexandria, Cairo with a surface area equal to Rome's but with a population of some 15 million inhabitants is like a city that comprises a melting pot of different cultures. The capital extends for over 35 kilometres along the eastern bank of the Nile, the historical stage of many sensational events. The Roman-Byzantine embryo citadel of Babylon that became the Arab Al-Fustat in the 7th century, and the Fatimid Al-Qahira in the 10th century, was transformed into Gran Cairo by Italian merchants, yet the different urban developments that followed on from each other did not blend into a whole.

Pharaonic Egypt, exiled to Giza and besieged by illegal building speculation, lies below the ancient Coptic quarters of the city of Saladin and the Mamelukes, whilst the opulent Baroque palaces of the rich trading middle class and the buildings, inspired by Haussman, spread out to the modern satellite town of Muhandisin. They also stretch to the royal residences of the two islands of Roda and Gezira (confiscated and transformed into museums), the large Art-Deco-style villas of Heliopolis and the non-descript buildings of the suburbs of Aguza, Muhandisin and Doqqi.

A cloud of smog mars the splendour of the largest city on the African continent, which presents a familiar image of big hotels, boutiques, European clothes, skyscrapers, and an unfamiliar metropolitan atmosphere that arouses conflicting feelings. The Levantine cul-

ture, the dirt, the crumbling buildings, the deafening noise, the chaotic traffic, the veiled women, the rickety pavements, the overhead roads and the overcrowding has led men to invade the areas set aside for the dead. Cairo is a Tower of Babel that comprises people, animals and cars over which tower the fine-stemmed minarets emitting their regular call to the faithful, the gilded domes echoing to the sound of prayer and the light marble carvings of silent mosques. Besides all this, Cairo, the meeting point between Arab and European cultures, is still what inspired also *A Thousand and One Nights*, the sophisticated city that gave the world a Nobel literature prize winner, Nabuib Mahfouz, and the world's oldest functioning university, Al-Azhar.

Islamic Cairo affords merely a vague idea of the splendour reached by the city under the Mamelukes. The great mosques, especially that of Ibn Tuloun, the oldest in the city and a masterpiece of world architecture, feature in this splendour. Built in the 9th century by Ahmed Ibn Tuloun and modelled along the lines of the Babylonian complex of Samarra and later transformed into a military hospital, salt warehouse and home for beggars, restoration in 1918 brought back its former magnificence. The large internal courtyard, the portico, the spacious grounds, the delicate gypsum decorations and the square-shaped minaret with spiral external staircase were rebuilt. The mosque complex of Al-Azhar, built in the 10th century, lies

60 top left and 60-61 To the south of the Citadel, in the huge southern cemetery of Cairo, which stretches over 550 hectares, are twelve burial monuments of the ancient Mameluke sultans, including the Mausoleums of Sudun (1504), es-Sawabi (1286), es-Sulnayina (1350),

Badr ed-Din el-Qarafi (1300) and Tanjkhizboga (14th century). The tombs of the Mamelukes assassinated by Mohammed Ali are in the small Hosh el-Basha cemetery, built in 1820, where the successors of Mohammed Ali are also buried.

at the centre of Islamic culture. With its 5 minarets, 300 marble pillars, 6 doors and the wide portico, it houses a prestigious university, with four Sunni orthodox faculties of jurisprudence and a library with over 60,000 tomes.

The mosques include the Madrasah (Islamic school) of Qalaun, built by the Mameluke sultan, Qalaun, at the end of the 13th century, with gypsum decoration, stained glass and decorated ceilings, the Fatimid mosque of Al-Aqmar (1125) located below street level, and the Mameluke mosque of Qaitbey (1472) with its elegant "beehive" stone facade. Also of great importance is the mid-fourteenth century mosque with tomb and madrasah of the sultan Hassan, with its 86-metre-high minaret and dome entirely faced on the inside in pure gold. The capital's many mediaeval and not just religious buildings can also be discovered and leave the visitor spoilt for choice. Those most worthy of note include the ancient caravanserai of Al-Ghuri, dating back to the early 16th century, which also houses a small handicraft museum, and Bab Al-Futuh, the Gate to Conquest, an interesting example of 11th-century mediaeval architecture.

Much of Cairo's history is enclosed behind the citadel's walls, which were started by Salah al-Din ibn-Ayyubi, the legendary Saladin of mediaeval fame, between 1176 and 1183, on a hill that was first the residence of the Mameluke sultans and then of the Ottoman pashas. Here among the mainly Ottoman buildings as well as the Mohammed al-Nasir

60 top right
The Nilometer on the island of Rhoda, built by the Umayyadi caliphs around 715, is similar to the one built by the ancient pharaohs and had the same purpose - to measure the level of the river for the setting of the tax rates.

61 top The mosque of Mohammed Ali, with its rich decorations, houses the tomb of the politician who had it built, within a gilded bronze enclosure. The dome of the mosque, 21 metres in diameter and 52 high, is covered in gilded reliefs and adorned with verses from the Koran.

61 right Also known as "The Alabaster Mosque", due to the precious materials used for the covering, the mosque of Mohammed Ali has two minarets and a clock tower, donated in 1846 by Louis Philippe as thanks for the obelisk of Place de la Concorde, in Paris, gifted to France by Egypt in 1833.

mosque of 1335 stands the massive mosque of Mohammed Ali, also known as the alabaster mosque (from the facing once on the walls). Built between 1830 and 1848 in Turkish style and decorated with European and Islamic motifs, its outside court-yard is embellished by a tower in which a baroque clock is set, a thanks-giving by the French for the Parisian obelisk in Place de la Concorde. Ancient Babylon dozes in the Old City, where the capital's Christian and Jewish monuments stand. These in-clude the monastery of Saint George, the Church of Saint Sergius, in the underground chapel of which the Holy Family is said to have sought refuge during their flight to Egypt, the Church of Saint Barbara, both re-built several times, and the synagogue of Ben Ezra, with its beautiful stained glass and a 6th-century Torah.

As with the buildings, the museum collections of Cairo continue to provide a separate picture of Egyptian civilization and culture. Inside the walls of the Coptic museum are the remains of the bastions of the ancient Fortress of Babylon and the artistic evidence of the Christian faith in Egypt. The Islamic Art Museum boasts more than 75,000 articles of ceramic, glass, tiles and carved wooden objects related to the dominion of Islam. Antiquities and Ottoman handicraft are exhibited at the small Gayer-Anderson museum in a series of 6th and 7th-century homes, while the technical process of papyrus, the aquatic plant that encouraged the skill of writing and had such an enormous influence on Egyptian civilization, can be admired on the three boats anchored off Giza where the Papyrological Institute has its seat. The collection housed at the Egyptian Museum founded by August Mariette is naturally magnificent, and represents a triumph in terms of culture and visitors: all the best of ancient Egypt in more than 100,000 artefacts (and those are just the ones on display) from the bust of Queen Tiyi to the famous treasure of Tutankhamun.

From its former splendour to today's poverty, immigration, a demographic explosion and a lack of accommodation have forced its inhabitants to occupy Cairo of the dead. As well as four cemeteries, the capital also has two large necropolises at

62 right The Museum of Cairo, as well as its extraordinary treasures, also contains a great many statues. In this photo we see the colossal statue of the pharaoh Merenptah, the successor to Ramses II (19th dynasty).

63 This married couple in painted limestone were found in a tomb on the site of Meidum. The couple in question are Prince Rahotep, high priest of Heliopolis and son of Sefru, and his wife Nophret.

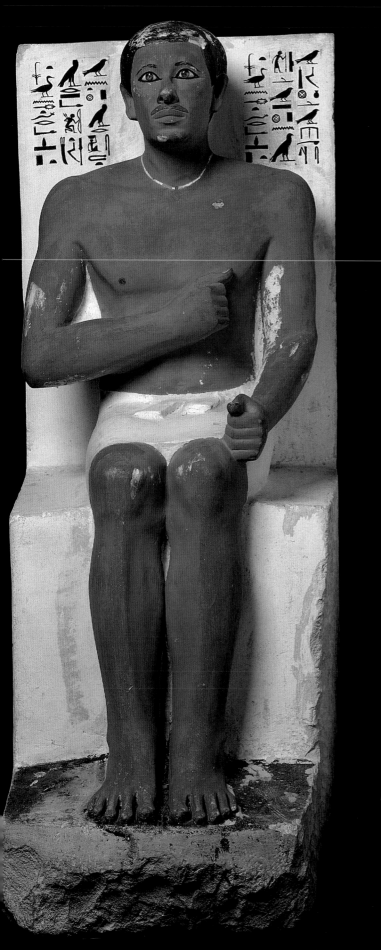

the foot of the Mokkatam hills with more than 200,000 inhabitants, of which a tenth actually reside in the ancient Mameluke tombs. This has led to a densely populated area in which some important buildings are housed including the mosque-mausoleum of the sultan Barquq, (1414), the first of the Mamelukes, with two twin minarets and domes, the complex of sultan Barsbey, (1432), with dome and minaret and the Qaitbey mosque, (1472), a masterpiece of Mameluke art with its splendid dome in sculpted stone.

64 In this fine statue found in the north-western sector of the Ramesseum, we can recognise Merit-Amon, also known as the "white queen". This was the daughter and great royal wife of Ramses II.

64-65 top This painted wooden model shows 40 lancers of Assyut and was found in the tomb of Mesehti, a leading dignitary who lived around 2000 BC.

64-65 bottom The "Geese of Meidum", a wall-painting on a thin layer of sand and clay, was situated in a corridor in the tomb of Nephermaat, a burial that could date back to the start of the reign of Snefru, around 2620 BC.

65 top This model from the tomb of Meketra shows a fishing scene on the Nile. The fishermen, on board papyrus vessels, are hauling in a net full of fish.

65 bottom This wooden model was also found in the tomb of Meketra, a dignitary who lived at the end of the 11th dynasty, around 2000 BC. It shows the deceased seated beneath a portico with his son and some scribes, while he inspects and counts the herds pushed forward by the peasants.

66 top The great
burial chamber of the
pyramid of Kafre,
dug out from the
rock, with a ceiling
of superimposed
limestone slabs, was
found in 1818 by
Giovanni Battista
Belzoni of Padua,
who left a message
written on a wall to
bear witness to his
act. An empty
sarcophagus was
found in the chamber.

66-67 The pyramid
of Kafre, 136.5
metres high and
210.5 broad, still
retains its limestone
point. The sides are
inclined at an angle
of 50° and 20 seconds,
and the total volume
is in the region of
1,659,200 cubic
metres. The building,
constructed for the
son of Khufu, has two
north-facing
entrances.

67 top left
The complex of Giza
can be seen as the
symbol of Egypt itself.
The pyramids, situated
around ten kilometres
from Cairo, are on a
high rocky plain on the
western bank of the
Nile. The date of
construction of these
extraordinary
monuments, somewhere
around the middle of
the third millennium,
is still disputed.

67 top right
The pyramid of the
4th dynasty pharaoh
Khufu is 137 metres
high - originally, its
gilded point brought
it up to 147 metres -
with a total volume
of 2,600,000 cubic
metres. The stone
blocks used to build
it, slotted into place
with exceptional
precision, weigh
from 2 to 16 tons.

66 bottom Designed
as the tomb of
Cheops, the pyramid
of Khufu is reached
from a narrow
corridor that leads to
the burial chamber,
which measures 10.45
metres in length, 5.2
in width and 6 in
height.

A visit to Giza on the plateau beyond Cairo can have an unsettling effect on the tourist who has seen the Egyptian Museum and been dazzled by the remains of the past splendour of the country's two main cities, and yet is eager to witness first hand the pharaonic monuments. The beautiful tree-lined boulevard that once linked the city to the archaeological area has been replaced by a very ordinary road with two lanes, and the view of the most famous archaeological complex in the world has a very disconcerting effect.

The visitor's initial reaction is of disappointment at all the concrete and degraded environment surrounding the most famous monuments of antiquity. He then has to struggle through hordes of tourists, miles of buses, masses of cameras, the incessant buzz of camcorders, and fend off camel-ride touters and demands for baksheesh. In a state of grand confusion, having witnessed not the greatness of a country but the fact that it is a destination for mass tourism, the visitor has to give the colours, emotions, sounds and sights experienced time to settle, in order to restore the right balance between reality and his expectations. Only then, having freed his mind from preconceived ideas and the modern architecture surrounding the three pyramids of El Giza, and by imagining them solely in a desert setting, can he evoke a sense of the past and feel enthusiasm over their essential line and perfection.

The three awe-inspiring monoliths give only a vague idea of what these funerary complexes were at their origin; complexes that also included a temple, a small symbolic pyramid and a covered paved road connected to a religious building which ferried visitors from the Nile to the valley by means of a causeway that reached the foot of the monuments.

Considered the Seventh Wonder of the World, the pyramid of Khufu, a 4th-dynasty pharaoh, was immediately recognized as the largest of the three. 137 metres high (the limestone slabs that faced it and the golden tip that brought its height to 147 metres have disappeared), according to some Egyptologists it was built around 2500 BC, one of the most disputed dates in the history of archaeology. The technique used to build these ancient colossal monuments with blocks weighing from two to sixteen tons is also the subject of debate. This is an awe-inspiring thought when considering not just the period in which they were built but above all the accuracy right down to the last millimetre with which they were brought together. For Khufu's pyramid alone, with its sides facing in the direction of the points of a compass, and its perfect right angles (with a maximum error of alignment of one twelfth of a degree), almost 2,600,000 blocks, each a cubic metre, were arranged in 201 rows. Such a Herculean task was perhaps too great to have been carried out by the

use of traditional ramps alone. Originally used as a funerary construction, the pyramid is accessible by means of a narrow corridor that leads to the funerary chamber from the empty sarcophagus, whilst other subterranean passages are directed so as to determine the passing of Orion over a certain part of the sky. Nearby in an airtight chamber, parts of a narrow and elegant solar boat were found in 1954. Today it is preserved in a boat-shaped building of questionable taste. Made of cedar wood, 43 metres long, 6 metres wide and 8 metres tall, it is composed of 1,224 pieces joined together not by screws, but by rope and cord, that took ten years of work to reassemble. In the vicinities of the building, soon to be replaced as it cannot ensure perfect storage of the precious find, there should be a second boat that will be restored as soon as the new museum is ready. In addition to the pyramid of Menkaure, the smallest of the three at 66 metres high, whose sarcophagus went missing during a shipwreck off the Spanish coast, and the pyramid of Kafre, 136.5 metres high, still with its limestone tip and small funerary constructions for queens, princesses and dignitaries, on the way to the temple of the valley of Kafre, lies Giza's star attraction, the Sphinx.

On several occasions it has been covered in sand and parts of it have been ruined. In its paws it still has a granite slab that commemorates the dream of Tuthmosis IV. In the dream, the Sphinx asked the prince to unbury him. In exchange, the Sphinx would give him the Double Crown of Egypt, and this is in fact what came to pass. This lion with its human head carved from the plateau's rock has also sparked off fierce debate among archaeologists. Traditionally believed to be an effigy of King Kafre, the deep marks of erosion caused by water on its body, 57 metres long and 20 metres high, have led some archaeologists to predate its execution by many thousands of years.

68-69 Known as Abu-el-Hol ("father of terror") in Arabic, the Sphinx is situated 350 metres to the south-east of the great pyramid. It has the shape of a crouching lion with a human head wearing a crown with the cobra symbol. It is 57 metres long and 20 high, and represents the pharaoh Kafre like a big cat guarding his own burial complex.

69 top left As in the rest of the Giza complex, this human-headed lion sculpted in the rock of the plain has given rise to fierce disputes over its date of construction. The deep signs of erosion from the water on the body and the clear lack of proportion between the head and the rest of the animal have recently led some archaeologists to attribute it to a period many years before its traditional date around the time of Kafre. The damage to the face of the Sphinx, traditionally attributed to the soldiers of Napoleon, is in fact probably due to artillery practice by the Mamelukes.

69 top right
The giant head of the Sphinx measures 5 metres in height, with the ear alone measuring 1.37 metres. As Dominique Vivant Denon, one of the scholars who took part in the ill-fated expedition of Napoleon Bonaparte, wrote, "With a monument like this, there can be no doubt that art was at a high level of perfection".

70 top
The archaeological complex of Abu Sir - halfway between Giza and Saqqara - contains not only the remains of a sun temple of the 5th dynasty, but also 14 pyramids, most of them now in ruins. Only 4 - the pyramid of Sahura, the mastaba of Ptahshepses, and the pyramids of Niuserra and Nepherirkara - still retain traces of their ancient splendour.

70-71 The site of Dashur, 26 kilometres south east of Giza and 10 from Saqqara, contains two 4th dynasty pyramids (belonging to Snefru) and three pyramids from the 12th dynasty. The most curious of all the constructions in the complex is a rhomboid pyramid, here in the foreground. In the background is the red pyramid, the first true pyramid built in Egypt.

Little remains of Memphis, the first capital founded by King Menes on the western bank of the Nile approximately 30 kilometres from Cairo. Almost nothing remains of the massive temple of Ptah or of the embalming chambers of the sacred Apis bulls. A huge couchant limestone statue of Ramses II, more than 10 metres high, and a large alabaster sphinx weighing 8 tons can be admired.

71 left and bottom right Memphis, capital of the Ancient Kingdom, was founded by the pharaoh Menes according to tradition, the first sovereign of the 1st dynasty. 4.25

metres high and 8 long, the alabaster Sphinx of Memphis, kept in the open air in the local museum, in all probability dates to the period of Amenophis II or Thutmosis I.

71 top right The limestone colossus of Ramses II, 10.3 metres high (but originally 13 metres, as part of the crown and the lower part of the legs are missing), kept in a specially built modern

construction, is one of the most important remains of ancient Memphis. A second colossus in pink granite discovered in the zone was erected in the square in front of the station of Cairo in 1955.

72 top left
The necropolis of Saqqara, the biggest in Egypt, is well known for the burial complex of the pharaoh Djoser, first king of the 3rd dynasty.

72 bottom left
The mastaba of the functionary Mereruka, in Saqqara, was discovered in 1892

by Jacques De Morgan. 40 metres long and 24 wide, it is the most complex of its kind from the Ancient Kingdom. Its 32 rooms, including one with a life-size statue of the dead ruler, were also used for the burial of the wife and son of Mereruka, and are adorned with lively fishing and everyday scenes.

72 right
The pyramid of Meidum, near Riqqa, was probably built by the last king of the 3rd dynasty, Huni. Designed as a seven-step pyramid, it was extended and

transformed by Snefru into a regular pyramid. Its current appearance, without the limestone covering, is more similar to a three-storey mastaba with high inclined faces.

The ancient mortuary compound of Memphis, Saqqara (from the god Sokar, lord of farming), the largest in the country, is situated north-west of the city on an arid and un-even desert plateau. In this vast mortuary compound dating back to the Old Kingdom is the first stone construction of the country, the step pyramid of King Djoser, the first of the 3rd dynasty pharaohs.

Almost 60 metres high, and surrounded by a rectangular wall over a total of 15 hectares, it comprises six receding steps approximately two metres high, that follow an east-west direction, and is considered the forerunner of the Giza constructions. According to tradition, it was built around 2686 BC by the engineer, Imhotep, and is surrounded by various smaller constructions. It also stands alongside the remains of 4th and 5th dynasty pyramids, which are important because of their religious inscriptions, known as the Pyramid Texts, that embellish the interiors. Worthy of special mention are: the pyramid of Unas, the mastaba-type tomb of Princess Idut and those of Mehu, Mereruka and Ti. Prayers and funereal rites are revealed, and covering the walls of tombs are friezes and paintings portraying daily scenes of animals, military life, battle, farming, handicrafts and entertainment. Many of these tell of life and the conception of death of the ancient Egyptians.

The plateau of Saqqara also conceals other treasures such as the catacombs of the sacred ibis and the Serapeum corridors containing the tombs of the sacred Apis bulls. Dug out of the rock they contain great sarcophogi in granite, basalt and limestone, and were all pillaged in ancient times except for one. To open the Serapeum, its discoverer, the legendary Mariette, had to use dynamite. Inside, as well as the embalmed bulls, a statue of a golden ox in solid gold was found, and it is now in the Louvre.

72-73 The stepped pyramid, nearly 60 metres high and surrounded by a rectangular walled enclosure, has been attributed to Imhotep, who built it around 2686 BC. Imhotep, a court vizier and doctor, was later deified and identified with Aesculapius the Greeks god of medicine. He signed his work twice - on the base of a statue of Djoser and near the entrance in the walled enclosure.

73 top left Among the many tombs in the complex of Saqqara, we can distinguish that of Irukaptah, director of the royal slaughterhouses in the 5th dynasty. The burial complex, which also contains the tombs of 10 members of his family, is decorated with 10 multicoloured statues cut out of the rock and surmounted with scenes of butchery, from which it takes its name, The Tomb of the Butchers.

73 top right
The pyramid of Djoser is surrounded by various smaller constructions and a number of 4th- and 5th- dynasty pyramids, with their interiors rich in reliefs and paintings, like the one in the picture.

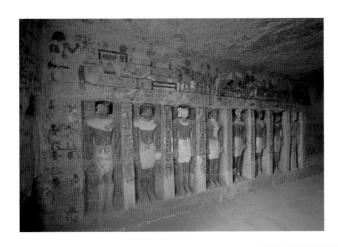

74 top Abydos, on the western bank of the Nile, is one of the oldest religious sites in Egypt. Here, according to tradition, the tomb of Osiris, God of the dead, was situated. The best preserved of the

religious buildings in the area is the great temple built by Sethi I, the "Memnonium" mentioned by Strabo. Built in limestone on sandstone foundations, the temple is unusual in its extension along a lateral wing.

74-75 The ruins of Medinet Madi, the Narmuthis of the Greek papyri founded by the rulers of the Middle Kingdom in Faiyum and extended by Amenemhat III and his son Amenemhat IV, contain the remains of a temple dedicated to the crocodile god Sobek, Horus and the goddess Renenutet, protector of the harvests and granaries.

75 top left The capital of the 15th nome of Upper Egypt, Hermopolis, also known as "The Hare", was dedicated to the baboon god Thoth. According to tradition, this was the place where the sun rose for the first time, and where the world was created. Among its most important

archaeological remains are the ruins of a basilica, a large covered market, a great temple of Thoth and a religious building dedicated to Amon-Ra.

75 top right Lake Qarun, also known as Birkat el-Kurun, or "the lake of the horn", because of

its shape, is 50 kilometres long and 12 wide. With an average depth of 4-5 metres, it is situated in the fertile region of Faiyum, 44 metres below sea level. Rich in large fish that live in the slightly salt water, it has attractive coves and banks covered in reeds.

74 bottom The tomb of Khnumhotep III, "Hereditary Lord", in the necropolis of Beni Hasan, contains rich decorations with scenes of everyday life, hunting, fishing, the arts and skills. Completely dug out of the rock, like the others in the cemetery, which contains 39 burials of great landowners, the tomb enables us to reconstruct a page in feudal history. In an inscription of 222 text columns, is a list of the ancestors of the deceased.

The fertile depression of the Faiyum area is then crossed; from here originate around 700 Roman portraits, which were placed on the mummies in place of the traditional funeral masks. One then passes the important necropolis of Beni Hassan, with the noble tombs of the Middle Kingdom dug into the rock. Those of Amenemhat and Khnumhotep III are of particular beauty. Finally, leaving behind the Graeco-Roman ruins of Hermopolis, the necropolis of the sacred ibis and the baboons of Tuna el-Gebel, the road leads to Middle Egypt. Little remains of the city of Tell el-Amarna, the capital of the heretic Akhenaton, on the eastern bank of the Nile. Destroyed in a climate of religious fervour after the death of the king, worship of the old gods was restored. Useful information on how life must have been comes from the necropolis. Digging into the rock to build it began in 1370 BC to house the tombs of the court dignitaries. There are many portrayals of the pharaoh and his family in the expressionistic style that became associated with Amarna. Akhenaton is no longer seen as a powerful giant sovereign who massacred his enemies, but is represented in the arms of his wife and holding his daughters in his arms. At Amarna tablets from the state archives containing the Amarna Letters between Akhenaton and his successors and the Asiatic, Palestinian and Syrian sovereigns were found by an elderly Bedouin. They had been buried by the sand that soon covered the city's few ruins.

Abydos on the western bank of the river is one of the most ancient places of worship in the country. It developed around the tomb of Osiris, god of the dead, and in addition to a series of burials and royal cenotaphs, it encloses the remains of temple complexes built by the pharaohs of the New Kingdom. One of the most outstanding of these cenotaphs for its beauty is that of Sethos I and is decorated with astronomical representations. Husband of Isis, alongside whom he ruled the world with fairness according to the legend handed down by Plutarch, Osiris was killed by his wicked brother Seth and dismembered. The faithful Isis wandered the land weeping in desperate search of her husband, whose body she finally managed to put back together. Osiris recovered to the extent that he was able to conceive a son, Horus. After having avenged his father, the young man succeeded and became Lord of the Underworld in governing the kingdom of the living. The first of the two temples of Abydos was built by Sethos I and finished by his successors is in limestone and sandstone. The colonnaded temple with courtyards, seven ornate shrines and two hypostyle halls became a destination in Roman times for sterile women and the ill in search of a cure. Its funerary chapels are embellished with the images of the voyage of souls of the dead, who crossed the Nile to gather around the tombs of Osiris. The complex of Ramses II, with its two hypostyle halls, stands out because of the incredible murals and a sculpted group in grey granite.

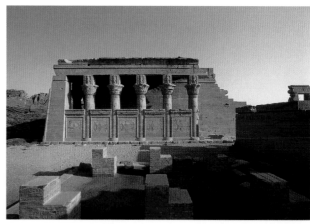

With the head (and often the body) of a cow, Hathor, goddess of love, mother of the gods and wife of Horus, was worshipped at Dendera, in the sandstone temple erected by the Ptolemies, who adopted her as their own from the Greek goddess Aphrodite. Rich in mural paintings and enclosed in a sacred wall with hypostyle hall, shrine, 11 chapels and 12 frescoed crypts, it boasts some beautiful Hathorian pillars that support an ornate ceiling with the signs of the Egyptian zodiac: Cancer, Gemini, Taurus, Aries, Pisces and Aquarius. Associated with the myth of Osiris, the sacred lake, enclosed by a rectangular wall and located near the temple, is one of the best preserved in Egypt. According to tradition, a relic of the dismembered body of the god was preserved in the city. During the great feasts of the god's resurrection, it was customary to deposit on the water a series of boats, each with a candle. At Dendera are the remains of two mammisi (temples of birth consecrated to the birth of the divine Harsomtus, son of Hathor and Horus), a Coptic basilica, a sanatorium and a small temple to Isis Hathor.

78 top
The photograph shows
the 20th-dynasty tomb
of Merneptah,
pharaoh and son
of Ramses II.
The picture shows
a detail of the
architrave of the door,
with the dual image
of the king as Osiris
welcomed by Anubis
and Harsiesis.

78 centre
The sarcophagus
of Horemheb, last
pharaoh of the 18th
dynasty, is in red
quartzite and was
found opened with
the cover split.
On the sides of the
sarcophagus we can
see the figures of some
of the gods that
protected the pharaoh.

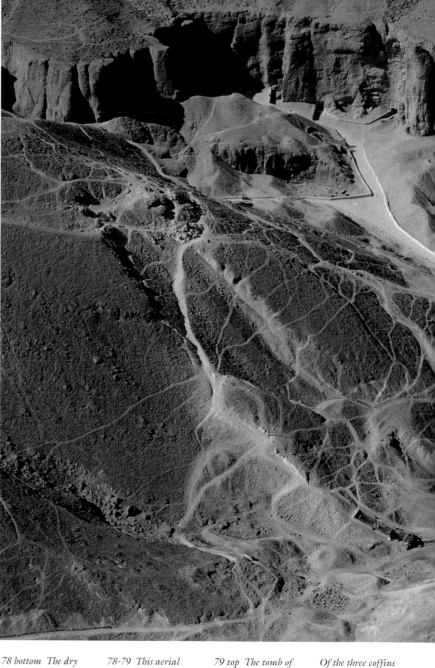

78 bottom The dry
climate has enabled
the extraordinary
paintings of the tombs
to retain their
original colours
almost intact. This
photograph of the
tomb of Horemheb
shows the pharaoh
taken by the hand by
Anubis, who is
holding the typical
attributes of the gods
- the uas *sceptre and*
the ankh *crown.*

78-79 This aerial
photo shows the Valley
of the Kings, the royal
cemetery of the
ancient Thebes which
housed the remains of
around 16 rulers
from the 18th and
19th dynasties. Here,
among others, are the
underground tombs
of Ramses II, Sethi I,
Amenophis II and
Thutmosis III, as well
as the famous tomb of
Tutankhamun.

79 top The tomb of
Tutankhamun,
discovered by
Howard Carter in
1922, is rather
compact and consists
of a corridor,
vestibule, sarcophagus
chamber (the only
decorated room) and
two storage rooms.

Of the three coffins
that contained the
remains of the
pharaoh, who died
young, only the one
in red quartzite
remains, decorated
with incisions from
religious texts, and
four funerary gods
at the corners.

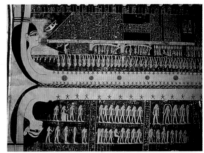

Luxor, the ancient Thebes, once capital of the country at the height of its splendour, certainly does not need any formal introduction. Here in a sort of open-air museum that occupies both banks of the Nile is the highest concentration of monuments in ancient Egypt. On the eastern bank lie the great Luxor and Karnak temples dedicated to Amon, whilst on the western bank in a narrow gorge stretches the necropolis with the famous Valley of the Kings, Valley of the Queens, the tombs of nobles and dignitaries and the great funerary compounds. Thebes of the dead comprises splendid funerary temples and vast hypogea (underground chambers) dug from twisting canyons. In a magnificent landscape of golden rocks, where the Nile is transformed into a Styx, lies the best of Egypt. Here, where silence has an eternal quality, the Valley of the Kings houses more than 60

79 centre and bottom Here we see the ceiling of the tomb of Ramses IV, one of the best preserved in the Valley of the Kings, also known as "the tomb of memtempsychosis".

The tomb, with the sarcophagus laid in the ground, contains a number of images from the Book of the Doors and the Book of the Dead, astronomical scenes and image of the sky by day and night.

80 top left The tomb of Nefertari Mery-en-Mut (literally "the most beautiful of all, loved by Mut") was discovered by Ernesto Schiaparelli in 1904 in the Valley of the Queens, the Theban cemetery on the left bank of the Nile. In this photograph we can see the east wall of the antichamber and the vestibule. Note the god Khepri to the left and Ra-Harakhti with Hathor-Imentet to the west, while the crossbeam is adorned with cobras and genii evoking eternity.

80 centre left The "great royal spouse" of the pharaoh Ramses II, Nefertari was without doubt the favourite out of the sovereign's many wives. In this picture, Nefertari is playing senet, a game similar to draughts, which symbolises the tests that the dead have to face in the kingdom of Osiris.

80 bottom left The tomb of Nefertari, with its complex plan and extraordinary wall paintings, is considered to be the most beautiful of all the burial structures in the Valley of the Queens. In this picture Nefertari, before Thoth, the divine scribe, is reciting magic formulas to obtain the pot and palette of the scribe and the powers connected with these two objects.

80 top right Due to preservation problems caused by water seepage, the tomb of Nefertari was closed for 40 years. In the Eighties, upon the initiative of the Egyptian Antiquities Organisation and the Paul Getty Conservation Institute, the restoration work began, and was completed in 1992. In the painting, the goddess Maat is shown with her wings outstretched in a gesture of protection.

80 centre right When it was discovered, the tomb of Nefertari had already been ransacked, and neither the body of the queen nor the rich burial treasure which had undoubtedly been present were found. In this picture, the queen presents ritual vases containing offerings to two gods - Hathor and Selkis.

80 bottom right The extraordinary beauty of the wall paintings, now brilliantly restored to their ancient splendour, show Nefertari led by the hand by the falcon-headed god Harsiesi.

81 left This extraordinary image shows Nefertari wearing a wig in the form of a vulture, surmounted by a plumed crown with the sun, a usekh-collar and an earring in the form of a cobra.

tombs (of which only around ten can be visited) mainly of the 18th- to 20th-dynasty pharaohs, from Sethos I (one of the finest) to Ramses III and Amenophis III, not to mention the famous burial chamber of Tutankhamun, found intact in 1922. Equally fascinating is the Valley of the Queens, south-west of the Valley of the Kings, where the bodies of the 19th- to 20th-dynasty queens and of the royal princes rest. These amount to approximately 80 tombs, including those of Queen Titi and Nefertari (wife of Ramses II, one of the richest in decorations and with an extremely complicated layout) and of Amonher-Khopeshef, son of Ramses III.

The dignitaries and officials of the New Kingdom, a period from which Thebes began to acquire importance, are buried in more than 400 hypogea lodged in the Valley of the Nobles, with the necropolises of Al-Asasif, Al-Khokha, Sheikh Abd al-Qurna and Qurnet Mura. Almost none of the tombs of Thebes escaped the ancient marauders, who cleverly tricked the royal architects and managed to get round traps, false corridors and defence systems, gaining possession of the treasures in them. To protect at least the mummies of their lords from this systematic pillaging, a handful of priests and faithful guards were forced to transfer them in secret from one tomb to another. They were finally gathered in the narrow well where Maspero found the remains of the main Egyptian sovereigns in 1881.

80

81 top right *The god Osiris, wearing the same tunic as Nefertari to indicate the assimilation of the queen and the god, appears four times in the tomb of the royal spouse, on pillars in the burial chamber.*

81 bottom right *This painting, which symbolises the union of the gods Ra and Osiris, evokes the theme of death and the daily rebirth of the sun.*

81

82 top In the Theban cemetery of Sheikh Abd el-Qurna, a number of illustrious tombs were found, rich in wall paintings that have taught us a great deal about everyday life in ancient Egypt. This picture shows the tomb of Nakht, "Astronomical Scribe of Amon", who lived under Thutmosis IV. The tomb contains rich decorations with scenes of agricultural life, such as the cultivation of wheat or the grape harvest, as well as fishing and hunting scenes.

82 centre In the tomb of Rekhmire, "Governor of the city and vizier" of the 18th dynasty, we can see the offering of tributes, including live animals, by foreign peoples.

82 bottom The tomb of Nakht shows an extraordinarily detailed banquet scene, with offerings of food and flowers to the deceased and his wife Tawi - here seen with a duckling in her hand - who had the title "Singer of Amon".

82-83 The tomb of the "Governor of the City and Vizier" of Amenophis IV, Ramose, contains decorations, many of them sculpted, of the very highest quality. One particularly fine scene shows the funeral procession of the deceased - in this picture we see two guests at the banquet - which was never placed in the tomb, as it probably went with the ruler when he moved from Thebes to Akhetaton, Tell el-Amarna.

83 top The tomb of Pashedu, "Servant in the House of Truth" from the Ramses period, situated in the Theban cemetery in the valley of Deir el-Medina, is well known for the scene of the deceased drinking from a stream beneath a palm heavy with fruit.

83 bottom The tomb of Menna, "Scribe of the Chiefs of the Lord of the two Lands of Upper and Lower Egypt", who lived during the reign of Thutmosis IV, is very well preserved. In this delicate painting, we can see a young daughter of Menna as she gathers lotus blossoms.

84-85 The tomb of Sennegem, "Servant in the House of Truth" from the period of Sethos I and Ramses II, is famous for the scene that shows the Fields of Iaru - the transposition of the green agricultural zones of the Nile Delta in the Afterworld - where the deceased and his wife sow, gather and plough.

85 top left In the tomb of Sennegem we can see a painting which presents the mummy of the deceased already in the sarcophagus above the burial bed. At his sides are two protector divinities in the form of falcons, Isis to the left and Nephthi to the right.

85 bottom left The wall paintings in the tomb of Sennegem, with their unmistakable ochre background, are the finest in the necropolis of Deir el-Medina. The photograph shows one of the 8 scenes in the ceiling of the tomb.

85 top right This scene in the ceiling of the tomb of Sennegem shows the deceased and his wife Inyferti as they worship 5 stellar divinities.

85 centre right The tomb of Sennefer, a high-ranking functionary during the reign of Amenophis II, who lived in the second half of the 15th century BC, is situated on the south-eastern slope of the hill of Sheikh Abd el-Qurna, and is distinguished from the other tombs by the fact that the decorations in the burial chamber do not, as is normally the case, show the world beyond, but rather the deceased himself and his wife Meryt. This picture shows the boat used to haul the barge of Sennefer, on his return from the ritual journey to Abydos.

85 bottom right The deceased and his wife are portrayed first in the conventional way, seated on their chairs, then standing as they prepare to go out into the daylight, symbolically facing the door of the burial chamber.

87 top In the shrine to Hathor in the temple of Hatshepsut, we can see columns with Hathoric capitals, adorned with images of the goddess Hathor with the typical cow's ears.

87 bottom The lower shrine in the temple of Hatshepsut is dedicated to Anubis, the jackal-headed god. In this picture we can see the colonnaded room with 12 grooved columns and the entance to the two rooms that follow.

86 top left
The temple of Hatshepsut at Deir el-Bahari is in western Thebes. In the photo, showing the bas-reliefs of the naval expedition on behalf of the queen to the mysterious land of Punt, we can see a number of incense trees as they travel on board the ships.

86 top right
The upper terrace of the temple of Hatshepsut has a portico with pillars decorated with the remains of the colossal Osiric statues of the queen, mostly destroyed during the reign of Ramses III. The destruction of the complex began with Thutmosis III, the king whose throne had been usurped by Hatshepsut. Daughter of Thutmosis I, she took up the regency for her nephew Thutmosis III on the death of her brother Thutmosis II, then went on to proclaim herself queen.

86-87 Considered sacred to the goddess Hathor, the complex of Deir el-Bahari saw the construction of three burial temples, those of Mentuhotep (left), Thutmosis III (centre) and Hatshepsut (right).

In the lower floor of the funerary temple of Ramses II, there are some remains and a gigantic statue of the pharaoh. At Deir el-Bahari, with terraces perching over the precipitous walls, is the impressive and temple of the 18th-dynasty Queen Hatshepsut. The daughter of Tuthmosis I, for years the sovereign was co-regent with her nephew Tuthmosis III, although she effectively ruled on her own. Upon her death, he sought to erase all memory of her, having her name and effigies defaced from all the monuments. Also worth visiting are the remains of the funerary temple of Sethos I, completed by his son Ramses II, the temple of the 11th-dynasty King Mentuhotep I, also at Deir el-Bahari, and those of the Ptolemaic temple of Deir el-Medina. Further south are the ruins of the village of Medinet Habu with some buildings. These include the temple of Ramses III, the peripteral temple called "of the 18th Dynasty", the chapels of the Divine Adoratrices of the god Amon and various temples.

The only remains of the funereal temple of Amenophis III are the colossi of Memnon, standing more than 18 metres high. According to legend, one of the statues would sing at dawn, and in this way the god slain by Achilles would greet his mother Aurora. This was probably a sound emitted each morning when the stone started to dry off its night-time humidity, and was most likely the effect of damage caused by an earthquake in 27 BC before its restoration in the 3rd century under Septimus Severus.

*88 top left and centre
The burial temple of
Ramses II in Western
Thebes, also known as
the Ramesseum,
retains only a few
traces of its original
splendour. The
structure originally
contained two
spacious courtyards,
each with a
monumental
entrance, a great
colonnaded hall and
three smaller
colonnaded rooms,
a four-columned
sacristy, and various
crypts, storerooms and
annexes.*

*88 bottom left
In the Ramesseum,
as in many of the
other buildings from
the period of Ramses
II, there are
numerous portraits
of the pharaoh.
We can see the effigy
of the famous king
who reigned for 67
years in the Osiric
colossi and the colossal
statues, today seriously
damaged. This photo
shows a splendid
granite head which
belonged to one of the
two statues of the
pharaoh at the sides
of the main stairway
that led to the
colonnaded hall.*

88 right In this aerial photograph we can see the Theban mountain in the background and, in the foreground, the area occupied by the temple of Amenophis III, with the two gigantic statues known as the "Colossi of Memnon".

88-89 The cultivated land fertilised by the Nile abruptly gives way to the desert and the Theban necropolis. In this impressive photograph, we can see the Ramesseum in the foreground and the temple of Medinet Habu in the background.

89 top The Colossi of Memnon, 16.60 metres high and sculpted out of blocks of quartzite, face east and show the pharaoh Amenophis III. These were erected at the sides of the entrance to the funerary temple of the pharaoh, now completely destroyed.

90 The temple of Medinet Habu was built on the site where, according to tradition, the god Amon appeared for the first time. The complex, surrounded by a bare brick enclosure, contains the great temple of Ramses III, a smaller religious building constructed during the 18th dynasty, the remains of the royal palace and the funerary shrines of the divine worshippers of Amon. In the pictures we can see the first pylon (above) of the temple of Ramses III, 63 metres long and 20 high, the Ptolemaic pylon of the 23rd-dynasty temple (centre) and the second courtyard of the temple of Ramses III with the portico adorned with Osiric colossi (below).

90-91 Considered one of the most grandiose complexes of Theban religious architecture, the temple of Medinet Habu covered an area of 8 hectares and 62,626 prisoners worked on it.

91 top left The bas-reliefs on the pylons of the temple of Ramses III are famous, and this one, on the first pylon, shows the king hunting the wild bull in the swamps.

91 top right
The square columns
of the second
courtyard in the
temple of Ramses III
at Medinet Habu
are decorated with
scenes showing the
pharaoh presenting
offerings to the
goddesses, and several
traces of the original
colour remain.

92 top left The temple of Luxor, on the right bank of the Nile, is an eloquent example of the splendour of ancient Thebes. The complex, 260 metres by 50, contains a sanctuary preceded by a portico and colonnade, built under Amenophis III, while Ramses II ordered the construction of the entrance pylons, flanked by statues of the pharaoh and obelisks, and the first courtyard.

92 right and 93 top right The passageway that leads from the first courtyard to the colonnade of the temple of Luxor is guarded by two colossal statues, originally built by Amenophis III, the initiator of the great complex and usurped, as was his wont, by Ramses II.

92-93 65 metres wide, the entrance to the temple of Luxor, built by Ramses II, is flanked by two of the six original grey granite colossal statues of the pharaoh seated. These are 15.6 metres high, and were originally preceded by two obelisks, one of which was donated to Louis Philippe by Mohammed Ali.

On the other bank of the Nile at Luxor lies Thebes of the living, a holy city, sacred to the god of gods, Amon, the sun-god, occasionally depicted with the head of a ram. The city is also sacred to his wife Mut and son Khonsu, and many examples bearing witness to its ancient glory remain. "No city under the sun was so rich in splendid gold, silver and ivory monuments or so many colossi and obelisks made from a single stone". This is how Diodorus Siculus described Luxor in 57 BC. In spite of the plundering that went on at the advent of Christianity and the damage inflicted by time, the eastern bank of the Nile still offers ample witness of the past, including the exhibits and sculptures in the local archaeological museum. The great temple of Luxor, measuring 260 by 50 metres, a setting for great holy feasts, has the traces of devotion of different sovereigns, especially Amenophis III and Ramses II. Connected in ancient times by a road almost three kilometres long, flanked by sphinxes, to the nearby temple of Amon-Ra at Karnak, is a sanctuary preceded by a peristyle and a colonnade built by Amenophis III. The great pillars at the entrance flanked by huge colossal statues of the pharaoh, obelisks and the first courtyard were the work of Ramses II. On an embankment near the south east side of the first entrance hall lies the ancient Fatimid mosque of Abu el-Haggag, which, in all probability, hides other remains of the temple.

93 top left The great temple of Luxor was connected to the nearby temple of Amon-Ra by an avenue of sphinxes with rams' heads. In the final stretch, these were replaced with human-headed sphinxes under the pharaoh Nectanebos I.

Approximately three kilometres from Luxor lies Karnak, a holy city with walls behind which are preserved the impressive ruins of sacred buildings. One of the most important is the great temple of Amon built under the 12th-22nd dynasty pharaohs, comprising vast interiors, (feasting rooms, shrine, large hypostyle hall, sanctuary and wide courtyards). The ruined temple of Ptah has five doors, a porticoed courtyard and shrine with three chapels, while the temple of Khonsu, the moon-god, has a great entrance, hypostyle hall, courtyard and shrine. Only bare ruins remain of the temple of Montu, the temple of Opet with its terrace, vestibule and various smaller rooms, and those of Mut, built by Amenophis III, Ramses III. A series of small temples, a holy lake, massive pillars decorated with colossal statues and two lines of sphinxes complete the complex.

96-97
The Ptolemaic temple of Khnum, the ram-headed god and creator of humanity, in Esna has a spacious colonnaded hall dating to the reign of the emperor Claudius, with 24 imposing columns holding up a ceiling decorated with astronomical scenes and signs of the zodiac.

97 bottom centre
The temple of Kom Ombo, built in the Ptolemaic period, is dedicated to the crocodile god Sobek and Haroeris, with the head of a falcon. The building, whose plan is almost identical to that of the temple of Edfu, has two entrances, with pylon, a courtyard, two colonnaded rooms, one of which is the front portico, three vestibules and two sacristies.

*96 top left
The Graeco-Roman temple of Esna contains a number of elegant bas-reliefs with magical rites, images of Roman emperors dressed in the Egyptian style and making sacrifices to the gods, and battle scenes with Domitian and Trajan.*

96 top right and 101 top The temple of Edfu, the ancient capital of the second nome of Upper Egypt, is dedicated to the god Horus, protector and divine image of the pharaoh. Begun in 237 BC and completed in 57 BC under the Ptolemaic pharaohs, this is one of the best preserved in the country. 137 metres long and with a maximum width of 79 metres, enclosed within its walls, it consists of a pylon, great courtyard, portico, two colonnaded halls, two vestibules and a sacristy with shrines.

Unlike us, the ancient Egyptians did not head north, but south from where the great river that was the lifeblood of the country had its source. Up the Nile towards Aswan, the stream of water becomes narrower and the vast plains gently merge into hills. The compact Ptolemaic temple of Khnum, the god with a ram's head and the creator of humanity, was shaped by the river's silt on a lathe, and is besieged by the modern Isna, known for its many locks. It boasts a great hypostyle hall with 24 impressive pillars, many of which are of a different type. In particular, the bas-reliefs depicting Roman emperors dressed in Egyptian style, intent on making sacrifices to the gods, are exquisite. The bas-reliefs compete in beauty with those of the Horus temple at Edfu, capital of the second nome in Upper Egypt, known as Apollinopolis Magna to the ancient Greeks. The Horus temple was begun in 237 BC and ended in 58 BC under the Ptolemies, and is one of the best preserved in the country. Equally important is the Ptolemaic temple of Kom Ombo (the ancient Nebet) dedicated to Haroeris and to Sobek, the crocodile god, adored as bride and son. The building has two separate entrances that lead to the two sanctuaries whilst the pillars are decorated with flower capitals from the Ptolemaic period. In its surroundings, as inside the complex, hundreds of embalmed crocodiles were found, whilst in all probability one was kept in the small square tub that decorates the courtyard.

On the same latitude as Hong Kong, the city of Aswan, 900 kilometres south of Cairo, boasts a unique monument, the Hotel Pullman Cataract (formerly the Old Cataract), with a splendid dining-room and a great dome in Mameluke style. The city is also home to the ancient tombs of the Elephantine nobles dug into the rocks of the Gharbi Aswan escarpment, the Aga Khan Mausoleum and the ancient Coptic monastery of Saint Simeon, abandoned in the 13th century. Rommel, Churchill, British royalty and Farouk I were all guests at this centre, inaugurated in 1899, and kept alive the area's tradition of tourism. A frontier city, Aswan offers a stopping point along the great river. Controlled by a series of

dams, the Nile becomes a calm placid lake dotted with a series of islands. Like smooth, stone hippopotami bathing in the river, the round guano-striped rocks of the Elephantine Island turn red or black according to the light. This is the largest of the islands that break the monotony of the panorama, and they are a pleasure to watch. Less than two kilometres long and half a kilometre wide, the island has a palm-grove, the remains of some temples, a small archaeological museum, the striking cylindrical tower of the Hotel Oberoi and the old Nilometer, a flood warning instrument used to calculated the floods. A huge botanical garden takes up most of Kitchener's Island and has many species of plants from Africa and Asia.

98-99 The white sails of the feluccas punctuate the waters of the Nile at Aswan, the town built on the right bank of the great river.

99 top In Aswan, 900 kilometres south of Cairo, we find the ancient tombs of the nobles of Elephantina, as well as the red sandstone mausoleum in which Aga Khan, chief of the Ishmaelites, is buried.

Beyond Aswan, the terminus of the valley of the Nile in Upper Nubia, the river is no longer navigable and is en-
gulfed by Lake Nasser. This was formed
by the huge dam that has had such an
influence on the area's environment,
also causing the spread of bilharziosis, a
dangerous parasite infection. In Nubia,
the ancient crossroads between Egypt
and Africa, which has disappeared because of the lake, there were more than
23 temples and sanctuaries that have
been taken to bits and rebuilt else-
where. This is what happened to the
monuments of the Philae Island, which
were transferred to the Agilika Island,
the pavilion of Nectanebo I, the temple
of Isis, the small temple of Hathor and
Trajan's pavilion.

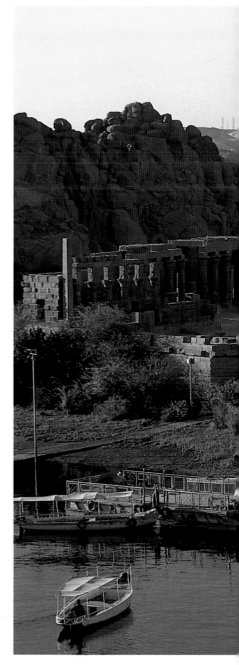

100-101 Many temples of ancient Nubia which would have been submerged after the formation of Lake Nasser, were dismantled and reassembled in safer locations. This was the case with the monuments once standing on the island of Philae, transferred to the island of Ajilka, which was levelled and extended for the occasion.

101 top left The dismantling and re-assembly work on the temples of Philae, carried out by the Egyptian government with the assistance of Unesco, began in 1972 and was completed in 1980. As well as the pavilion of Nectanebos I, the temple of Isis, the small temple of Hathor, a nilometer and the pavilion of Trajan were moved to the island of Ajilka.

100 left The pavilion of Trajan on the island of Philae, situated on one side of the temple of Hathor, has a portico with 14 bell-shaped columns. The building, used for the complex rituals linked with the cult of the goddess, was left unfinished.

100 right and 101 top right The temple of Isis of Philae is the largest of the religious monuments built on the island. It consists of a monumental entrance, a temple of birth dedicated to Isis the Elder, a second pylon, a colonnaded room with 10 columns and a portico with 12 shrines, a crypt and various other areas, including a terrace with the funerary shrine of Isis. On the eastern wall of the portico is the bilingual decree of Ptolemy V Epiphanes, which also appears on the famous Rosetta Stone.

102 top and 102-103
The temple of Dakka,
built during the
Graeco-Roman
period, was
consecrated to Thoth.
Begun under Ptolemy
II Philadelphos by the
king of Ethiopia
Hergamenes (3rd
century BC) on the
site of an older temple
from the New
Kingdom, this consists
of a pylon, three floors
of rooms, two terraces,
portico and vestibule.

102 centre
About a kilometre
to the south of the
High Dam of
Aswan, near the
western shore of Lake
Nasser, are the
remains of the
Nubian temple
of Mandulis, or
Kalabsa. 71.6 metres
long and 35.5 wide,
this was dismantled
and rebuilt using the
funds set aside by
West Germany.

102 bottom
The temple of Kalabsa
was built under
Augustus on an older
building from the
period of Amenophis
II, and has a similar
plan to that of the
temple of Edfu, with
pylon, courtyard,
portico on three sides,
and three-roomed
pronaos and naos, all
enclosed within double
walls.

103 top left
Dismantled and
rebuilt nearly four
kilometres to the west
of the original site
with the financial
contribution of the
United States, the
temple of Wadi es-
Sebua, 140 kilometres
south of Aswan, was
dedicated to Amon-Ra
and Ra-Hermakhis,
and consists of a pylon
followed by courtyard,
portico, vestibule and
a number of shrines.

103 top right
The religious complex
of Hamada, which
also includes the temple
of Derr and the tomb
of the governor Pennut,
is dominated by the
religious building
dedicated to Amon-
Ra and Ra-Harakhti
by Thutmosis III and
Amenophis II.
Considered one of
the finest Nubian
examples, its transfer
was funded by
contributions from
France.

The final visit on a trip to Egypt has to be the temples of Abu Simbel located at southernmost points of ancient Egyptian civilization along the Nile. These date back to Ramses II's rule, and are among the most spectacular remains of antiquity. The Great Temple stretches deep into the rock from which it is cut for almost 60 metres. Its facade bears four seated statues, more than 20 metres high, on thrones, and depicting the pharaoh surrounded by smaller images of his mother, wife and sons. Inside are an entrance, a central hall flanked by eight statues of the king in two rows and decorated with friezes illustrating the sovereign's military campaigns. Naturally smaller is the nearby temple dedicated to his wife, Nefertari (also known as the temple of Hathor) with its facade embellished by six statues, 12 metres high, of the royal family, with entrance, shrine and hypostyle hall.

The fame of both monuments derives not so much from their great beauty but from the events they have withstood. Condemned to certain destruction by the rising water of Lake Nasser, they were sawed up and carried up the hillside to be rebuilt well above water level. In 1960 for over ten years Unesco had the 300,000 tons of the temples' sandstone solidified by resin injections, cut into 1,036 blocks and set into two artificial concrete hills, with the monuments in their original direction. Twice a year, on 20th October and 20th February, this direction enables the sun to illuminate three (Amon, the deified Ramses and Harmakhis) of the four statues placed in the Great Temple's shrine. The fourth, Ptah is taken from the realms of Greek mythology. Beyond Abu Simbel, the lifeblood of Egypt separates into the White Nile and the Blue Nile at Khartoum. It covers a further 5,600 kilometres over a harsh land that is difficult to reach, and flows into the heart of the African continent to its source, the river Kagera, the longest tributary of Lake Victoria. The discovery of this source was one of the greatest mysteries of its time, and was to cost a great deal in terms of pain and suffering, together with the loss of many human lives. But that is another story.

105 top right
The portico of the great temple, 18 metres long and 16.7 wide, contains eight Osiric statues of Ramses II, 10 metres high. In those resting against the south wall, the pharaoh is wearing the white crown of Upper Egypt, and in those of the north wall he wears the red crown of Lower Egypt.

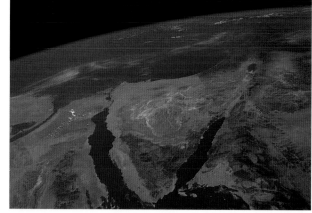

*B*reathtaking landscapes and a history full of mysticism are what this region has to offer. Moving away from the banks of the Nile means leaving behind the monumental pomp of pharaonic buildings for the austere seclusion of small convents barricaded around churches with golden interiors, and small patches of garden saved from the desert. It also means admiring hazy horizons that merge into one another under a blinding light, capitulating before the seductive softness of gently sloping dunes, absorbing the strong colours and vast space, which is varied yet the same. Rough, dusty roads and rail tracks smelting in the sun create an umbilical cord that goes to the interior of the arid Sinai peninsular, inhabited mainly by Bedouins and full of harsh solitary mountains up to 2,000 metres high, that gently transform into the chic and lively Red Sea resorts with their ultramodern hotels.

An Asiatic appendix to Egypt, which attracted the pharaohs for its wealth of copper mines and precious stones (made even more precious by recent discoveries of oil and manganese beds), the peninsular has almost always been under the control of the Egyptians. Once past the tunnel dug under the Suez canal dedicated to General Ahmed Hamdi, who fell during the 1973 Arab-Israeli war, starts the pilgrimage through the many places supposed to have been the scene of events in Exodus. One of them, which is said to be known to Moses, is the Uyun Musa oasis, with its small wells of salt water made drinkable - according to tradition - by a piece of wood cast by the Biblical hero.

106 left
The indigenous Bedouin still make up the majority of the 200,000 inhabitants of the Sinai Peninsula, most of whom are concentrated in the northern coastal plain.

106 right In this satellite photograph we can make out the triangular shape of the Sinai Peninsula, with the Gulf of Suez to the west and the Gulf of Akaba to the east.

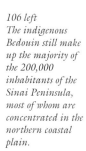

106-107 This photo shows the oasis of Ain Umm Ahkmed, in the Sinai. This arid peninsula, an outcrop of Asia in Egypt, was much favoured by the pharaohs for its copper mines and deposits of precious stones.

107 top left Built between 1859 and 1869 by the Universal Maritime Canal Company of Suez to connect the Mediterranean and the Red Sea, the canal, 161 kilometres long, is considered one of the greatest works of engineering of the 19th century.

107 top right The temple of Serabit el-Khadem, in the Sinai peninsula, is dedicated to Hathor, goddess of turquoise.

Than there are the *hammam faraun malun* or "baths of the cursed pharaoh", which are sources of hot sulphuric water that gurgle at the feet of the Hammam Faraun mount, where the pharaoh's army, chasing the Hebrews, was swallowed by the waters. From the oasis of Feiran, dominated by the Gebel Tahuna, the mount from which Moses prayed for his people during combat with the Amalecites, to the Er-Rahah plain, where the Chosen Race was to camp, the many holy places of the Sinai prepare the visitor for the most famous of them all, the Greek Orthodox monastery of Saint Catherine. Built in the first half of the 6th century by the emperor Justinian on the biblical site of the Burning Bush, on a mountain, at a height of 1,570 metres, it is a real fortress, measuring 84 by 74 metres, surrounded by a granite wall built between A.D. 527 and 565 with slits and a watch tower 12 to 15 meters high and up to 1.65 metres thick. Considered the most ancient monastery still in operation, it houses a valuable testimony of faith and culture, and until the Middle Ages, it was defended by only one point of access, a system of pulleys.

The monastery, inhabited mostly by Greek monks, is the result of a union of buildings from various periods: from the 10th-century mosque to the ancient Byzantine church of Transfiguration. It holds a vast collection of splendid icons, a large mosaic with apostles and prophets, two precious relics of Saint Catherine and images of the Byzantine

emperors Theodore and Justinian (who transferred to the surrounding village almost 200 Bosnian families to defend the monastery). It is also the site of the Burning Bush and is decorated with Blue Arabian ceramics. A striking feature is its central nave, where the sun and moon painted on the vault, when struck by the light of the corresponding star on 25th March, illuminate with their reflection the high altar. The monastery has a vast collection of treasures composed of ancient chalices, icons, mitres and enamels. Equally precious is the treasure represented by the library, which houses the most important collection of ancient volumes in the world, (second only to the Vatican): 3,500 Greek, Arab, Syrian, Armenian, Georgian, Coptic and Slavic manuscripts as well as many volumes and documents. The famous 4th century biblical manuscript, the Codex Sinaiticus, now in the British Museum, was also held here. The names of the pilgrims who, from the 14th to the 18th century, overcame hardship and danger to pay homage to the saint, are engraved on the richly frescoed refectory walls, whilst the bodies of the priests and monks rest in the Skull House in the centre of the monastery's garden, where espalier vines now grow.

The Mount named after Saint Catherine, also known as Gebel Katherina, is the highest in the land at 2,637 metres, and stands in the monastery's vicinities. Tradition has it that the body of the young Ecaterina, martyred at Alexandria under Emperor Maximinius (309-313), was carried here by the angels. Found by

monks, it is supposed to have been transferred by them to the convent later dedicated to her. Topped by a small chapel, the mount houses the convent of the six apostles and the 40 martyrs built in memory of the 40 monks slaughtered by Bedouins.

Southern Sinai also has other sacred mounts, related to the almost 40 years of pilgrimage by the Hebrews, as told in the Book of Exodus. The foremost of these is the Great Gebel Musa (2,285 metres high), Mount Sinai, where Moses is said to have received the tablets of the ten commandments. The mount can be reached by two different staircases (the second consists of 3,000 steps) cut into the granite by the monks. Along the climb one encounters the fountain where, according to tradition, Moses allowed his flock to drink. There is also a chapel dedicated to the Virgin and the great amphitheatre named after the 70 Elders of Israel, where the Hebrew notables are said to have gathered. The hermitage of Saint Stephen is hidden among the cypress trees and further up lie the remains of an ancient church built by Justinian (incorporated into the chapel in 1934) and a small mosque. Whilst Christians chose mountain peaks to worship their God, the pagans continued to sleep on their slopes. At Sarabit el-Khadim the little temple dating back to the Middle Kingdom dedicated to Hathor, goddess of turquoise, is partially dug into the rock. A series of offerings left by miners and workers bears witness to the trading importance of this area, so rich in turquoise mines, exploited be-

110 In this impressive photograph, we can recognise the site of Jebel Fuga. The Sinai Peninsula, known since antiquity for its mines, contains curious rock formations and extraordinary natural landscapes. The columns emerging from the sandstone, very likely fossil plant stems, have given this area the nickname "Forest of Columns.

110-111 The Sinai, the only land link between Africa and Asia, contains an imposing massif in the southern part of the peninsula, culminating in the mountain of St. Catherine's, Jebel Katherina, 2,637 metres high, and Jebel Musa, the Mountain of Moses, 2,285 metres. These mountains became holy places, linked to the Jewish and Christian religious traditions.

tween the Middle and New Kingdom. Since ancient times, vast mountainous areas of the Sinai and Arabic Desert supplied material for temples and palaces built upon the whim of a pharaoh or emperor. The stone mines of Gebel Hammamat dating back to the Old Kingdom, the emerald mines of Wadi Sedait, the auriferous mines of the Qift region and the Roman pentitentiaries located in the red porphyry and grey granite caves of Mons Porphyritis and Mons Claudianus, have always

enabled Egypt to depend on her own wealth of natural resources. The minerals of the Sinai extracted with flint-stone tools were put on board sailing vessels at the ancient port of Markha. The ruins of the village of miners at Maghara, one of the main mining centres of the Sinai, lie on a steep hill not far from the mine, to which it was connected by a double wall. Here were found stelas of Khufu and Snefru, tools and inscriptions, most of which have been transferred to the Cairo Museum.

112 top left Enclosed within its walls, the convent of St. Anthony was able to escape the Arab conquest, thanks to its isolated position in the Arabian Desert. After a long period of abandonment after being sacked by the Muslims in 1484, the complex was re-inhabited in the middle of the 16th century. Today it houses a community of Coptic Orthodox monks.

112 top right The richly frescoed convent of St. Anthony, surrounded by seven chapels, the cells of the monks, mill, grinding wheel and refectory, reflects the extraordinary intellectual life that flourished here between the 12th and 15th centuries, before the complex suffered the rebellion of its Muslim workers and was sacked and abandoned.

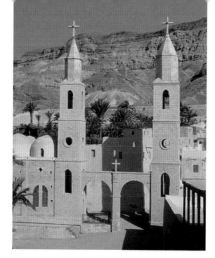

112-113
The monastery of St. Anthony the Abbot, in the Arabian Desert between the Nile and the Red Sea, was built between 361 and 363 by the disciples of the anchorite. Considered the father of the eastern monks, he died according to tradition aged 105, in the cave dug out of the rock wall of the hill 300 metres from the monastery, where he had withdrawn.

113 left Smaller and more modest than St. Anthony, the monastery of St. Paul in the Arabian Desert was founded in the 5th century. Sacked on various occasions, it was dedicated to the Theban hermit who died, according to tradition, aged 113.

113 top right In the church of the monastery of St. Anthony are several extraordinary Coptic frescoes showing saints, anchorites and archangels. Unfortunately, these precious works have suffered serious damage in the course of time.

113 bottom right Within its medieval walls, the monastery of St. Paul still contains three churches (St. Paul, St. Mercurius and a chapel-sanctuary built on the roof of the church of St. Paul) with frescoes in Coptic style showing the Virgin, the archangels and the Cavalier Saints George, Theodore and the Archangel Michael.

It was not just the mountain peaks that attracted Christians. The followers of the new religion also sought refuge in the isolation of the Arabian Desert, enclosed between the Nile and the Red Sea. This enabled them to escape from Islamic conquest. Such is the case of the monastery founded by St. Anthony's disciples between 361 and 363 in the place where the 3rd-4th century abbot, who hade become a hermit, lived by following the example of the other hermits in search of God and themselves. Considered the father of the monks of the Orient, according to tradition, he died aged 105. The saint would meditate in a large slit in the rock that can be seen on the hill slope close to the monastery.

Having flourished greatly between the 12th and 15th centuries, the religious compound was sacked in 1454 by Bedouin slaves and abandoned. The monks returned in the mid-sixteenth century and built a series of buildings enclosed in walls 12 metres high, with chapels, central tower, mill, oil-press and refectory, all grouped around a richly frescoed church. This complex was known for its ancient Coptic frescoes depicting hermits, saints and archangels, especially Gabriel and Michael, and has lost much of its original splendour. At Zafarana, not far away, is the monastery of Saint Paul built in the 5th century and sacked more than once. Having been abandoned and repopulated by the monks of the convent of Saint Anthony, it is dedicated to the hermit of Theban origin who, according to legend, died aged 113. The complex preserves its ancient mediaeval walls, the square tower and a set of buildings, including a library with ancient illuminated manuscripts. The three churches dominate the entire setting, the sanctuary chapel built on the roof of the sacred building, and the chapel dedicated to Saint Mercury. The ancient Coptic frescoes, obviously in a popular style, have many intricate decorations.

114 top In this photograph we see Naama Bay in Sharm el-Sheikh, a well known tourist resort on the Red Sea. Known only to sub aqua divers in the Sixties, this is now a favourite destination for hosts of tourists, for whom countless hotels and attractions of every kind have been built.

114-115 This aerial photograph shows the southern extremity of Sinai, Ras Mohammed. Declared a national park in 1989, this protected area is rich in wildlife both above and below sea level.

The lively Red Sea coast, striped with blood-red masses of a special seaweed, the *Trichodesmium erythraeum*, started to become a large tourist centre at the end of the Sixties because of its coral reef which attracted underwater fishing enthusiasts. It still preserves the remains of the ancient ports of Myos Hormos (Abu Shar el-Qibli), Leukos Limen (El-Quseir) and Berenice. Here the trade routes arrived from Koptos (present day Qift, in Upper Egypt) and led into the peninsular through Egypt, Sinai, Arabia and the neighbouring lands of Eritrea and Somalia at its tips. From there spices and perfumes came to the pharaohs and their court.

115 top Pharaoh's Island, "Jeziret Faraun", is situated a few kilometres from Taba, near the border with Israel. The island is dominated by a superb stone fortress, built in 1170 by Saladin. The imposing military complex, abandoned for years, was recently subjected to careful restoration.

115 centre The Bay of Dahab is another interesting tourist destination on the Red Sea, less crowded than Sharm el-Sheikh. The village, administrative and commercial centre of the zone was built by the Israelis.

115 bottom The natural park of Abu Galum is part of the territorial safeguard programme set up by the Ras Mohammed National Park authorities. This is an almost completely unspoiled area, far from the usual tourist destinations.

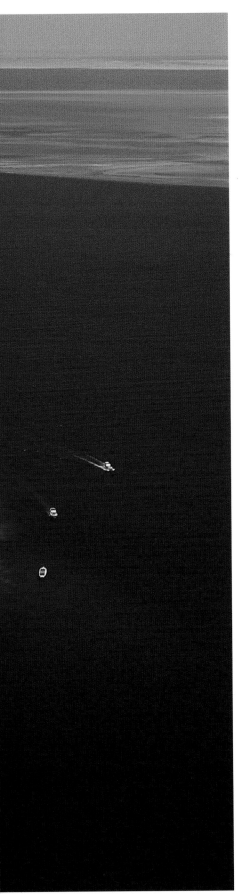

116-117 The islands
of Tiran, in the strait
of the same name that
separates the Gulf of
Akaba from the Red
Sea, are surrounded
by a sea that is
particularly rich
in fish and coral.

117 Many species
of coral live in the
waters of the Red Sea.
The imposing coral
reef offers food and
shelter to a great
variety of animals,
from the large but
placid mantas
(above) to these
terrible sharks
(centre) and the
elegant, solemn
batfish (below).

118 top *A group of butterfly fish with their brilliant yellow livery swim close to the coral reef, which was formed in the course of the centuries by communities of coral polyps.*

118-119 *Among the many marine species that find shelter in the ragged coral reef is the coral bass, splendid in its red livery with small blue patches.*

119 top With its warm waters, high salt content, lack of sediment and limited wave motion, the coral reef of the Red Sea is highly developed and hosts an extraordinary variety of living creatures - corals, sponges in all shapes and colours, sea anemones, molluscs and tiny invertebrates are gathered together here on the reef in a multicoloured, intricate harmony.

119 bottom The sun's rays filter through the blue surface of the sea, highlighting the delicate branches of an orange soft coral. However, you do not have to be an accomplished diver to appreciate the wonders of the Red Sea, all you need is a simple mask, a snorkel and a pair of flippers to reach this fantastic underwater world, inhabited by extraordinary creatures in every shape and form.

Monasteries, as well as the silent, austere ruins of temples and towering fortresses are even in the western oases, small areas of civilization that have been salvaged from the mortal grip of the desert, which covers 96% of the country west of the great river that separates the Libyan (or Western) Desert from the Arabic Desert. Here the sense of absolute peace dominates when in contact with the wilderness and creates and nourishes the religious oases with prayer and faith. Here it is easier to listen to the voice of God, to hear those of the ancient pagans and those created by the fear of men, the pharaohs and the Roman emperors. This is typical of the Kharga oasis, one of the hottest places on the planet, inhabited mostly by Nubians from lands submerged by the Nile after the building of the Aswan dam. Nestling in a broad valley approximately 200 km long and 20 to 50 km wide, here in the 6th century the army of the Persian Cambyses was decimated by the sand. The oasis was the scene of the contest between Ptolemies and Romans in leaving their mark on temples and monuments, and between 435 and 451 it was where Nestorius, patriarch of Constantinople, was confined after his schism. Once past the small archaeological museum and the modern, major city of Al-Kharga lies the temple of the city of Hibis. This is the only one left standing from the Persian period, and is the best preserved of all those built in the oases. It was built by Darius I and extended by Nectanebo II, the Ptolemies and fi-

nally by the Romans. Echoes of Christianity can be heard in the areas of Al-Bagawat, where a church and more than one hundred 4th- to 10th-century brick tombs stand, as do the neighbouring remains of the fortified convent of Qasr Ain Mustafa Kashif, a fortress of faith, unlike the military fortress of Ed-Deir with its towers and temple ruins. The ancient gods, however, had their triumph in the ruins of the three temples dotted along the southern route. Amon, Mut and Khonsu are honoured in Qasr el-Ghuata, the only religious building erected during the Ptolemaic era (250-280 BC). Amon of Ibis, or Amenebis, is however honoured in the temple, which remained a focal point until the Byzantine period from which stand the ruins at Ezba Qasr ez-Zaiyan.

122 top The oasis of Farafra, situated in the centre of a vast plain, is known for its inhabitants, who have the reputation of being skilful hunters. Completely surrounded by a stone wall and with a population of around a thousand, the oasis is the starting point for excursions into the White Desert.

122 bottom The fantastic limestone formations eroded by the wind of the White Desert 30 kilometres north of the oasis of Farafra are a blinding white.

122-123 The oasis of Siwa has numerous salt lakes and three hundred natural springs, such as the so-called "Baths of Cleopatra", a basin of water covered in musk. Situated near the border with Libya, the oasis was the site of the temple of Jupiter Amon, whose oracle confirmed the ascent to the throne of Alexander the Great in 331.

123 top left In this photograph we can see a typical house in the oasis of Siwa. The zone is now inhabited by around 10,000 descendants of the Berber tribe of the Zanatas.

123 top right Dakhla, with its 35,000 inhabitants, is the most highly populated of the western oases. Rich in archaeological finds, it contains the remains of Deir el-Hagar (the monastery of stone) and the Roman sandstone temple of Amon and Amonet in a small depression.

At Ezba Dush, on the southernmost edge of the oasis beside the ancient frontier stronghold built in the 4th century at the crossroads with Sudan, lie the remains of a temple to Isis and Osiris Serapis, which also has inscriptions by the emperors Trajan, Domitian and Hadrian. With its over 35,000 inhabitants spread out over around ten villages, the Dakhla oasis, 24 kilometres long and 45 wide, is the most densely populated and one of the richest in archaeological finds. Here one can find mastaba-type tombs dating back to the Ancient Kingdom of the Qila ed-Dabba necropolis, the remains of Neolithic settlements of Balat, the mediaeval quarter and fortified citadel of El Qasr, ancient capital of the oasis where ruins of the Roman temple to Amon and Amonet, known as Deir al-Hagar (the stone convent), survived an earthquake. Surrounded by a brick wall it has hieroglyphics with the names of Nero, Vespasian and Titus. Qaret al-Muzawaqa boasts richly decorated Roman tombs whilst Ahmeida preserves vague traces of former Roman splendour. Whilst the small oasis of Farafra in the centre of a vast stretch of level ground offers the spectacle of the bizarre wind-sculpted limestone formations of the White Desert, the mountainous land of Bahariya, dark because of its iron mineral-rich sand, has a series of ruins. Populated by some 26,000 inhabitants in the villages of Zabu, Mariya and Bawiti, to the west of the latter, it holds the ruins of an impressive Roman building in Doric style known as the Castle. It also has the ruins of three 26th-dynasty temples later appropriated by the Christians for their form of worship. At El-Heiz the continuous matrimony between Egyptian, Roman and Christian cultures is represented by the ruins of a Roman field and an ancient home facing a 5th- to 6th-century Coptic church dedicated to Saint George.

The green oasis of Siwa, with its lakes and thermal springs (more than 300), rises in isolation close to the Libyan border. Here, near the village of Aguermi, is the temple of Jupiter Amon, whose oracle Alexander the Great in 331 consulted and justified his rise to power. Of the great complex few traces remain: a few masses and a façade in Egyptian style, whilst the name of the most famous of the Ptolemies is heard at Ain El-Hamman in the "Baths of Cleopatra".

Although the western oases, with their mud houses that look as if they are about to melt under the first out-of-season rains, preserve the traces of the glorious past of the pharaohs and the religious fervour of the Christians, and the arid Sinai peninsular opens up to the scenarios of the mythical Biblical locations, and the scent that wafts through the air at Hurgada or Sharm el-Sheikh, where the new pharaohs roast under the sunshine, no longer evokes images of amber from the mythical land of Punt, but the more banal coconut oil, this does not mean that Egypt has lost any of its fascination in the eyes of the industrialized West, perennially in search of the exotic and mysterious. And here we have a mystery that not even a hundred Howard Carters would be able to solve. There will always be an Egypt in us.

INDEX

128 The great cycles of excavation carried out systematically under the supervision of the Egypt Exploration Society enabled us to obtain important information even from everyday objects, such as this painted wooden box, today kept in the Museum of Cairo.

Map by Betty Vandone